Manual on the Gospel of John

By Michael Penny

ISBN: 978-1-78364-490-2

Publications of the Open Bible Trust must be in accordance with the evangelical, fundamental and dispensational basis of the Trust. However, beyond this minimum, writers are free to express whatever beliefs they may have as their own personal understanding, provided their aim in so doing is to further the object of the Trust. A copy of the doctrinal basis is available from: -

THE OPEN BIBLE TRUST
Fordland Mount, Upper Basildon
Reading, RG8 8LU, UK.

www.obt.org.uk

First edition 1975
Reprinted 1978
Second edition 1987
Third edition 2014
Third edition revised 2018

****

All New Testament quotations are taken from the New International Version. (NIV) The Old Testament quotations are from the King James Authorised Version. (KJV, AV)

Unless indicated otherwise Scripture quotations are taken from the Holy Bible, New International Version Anglicised Copyright © 1979, 1984, 2011 Biblica. Used by permission of Hodder & Stoughton Ltd, an Hachette UK company. All rights reserved. 'NIV' is a registered trademark of Biblica UK trademark number 1448790.

Unless indicated otherwise Scripture quotations are from The Authorized (King James) Version. Rights in the Authorized Version in the United Kingdom are vested in the Crown. Reproduced by permission of the Crown's patentee, Cambridge University Press.

Manual on the Gospel of John

Contents

Page

Section 1:
- 4   Aims of this book
- 6   How to use this book
- 8   Why this book was written

Section 2:
- 11   Questions, with aids to the answers

Section 3:
- 28   Questions, answers and information on John's Gospel

Section 4:
- 123   Main themes of John's Gospel

- 130   More on John's Gospel
- 131   About the Author

SECTION ONE

1. AIMS OF THIS BOOK

It is easy to read a book but how much does one remember at the end? How much has one understood? This book is an *attempt to present some of the different ways of reading and studying suitable for different people*. It works through John's Gospel bringing out points the reader may have missed and explaining popular misconceptions. Thus, it also *hopes to stimulate thought and provoke discussion*. All in all, it hopes to meet the needs of a variety of people.

In working through John's Gospel we have *attempted to do three things:*

> **1. Show clearly the deity of the Lord Jesus Christ.**
> **2. Show that faith in Him secures eternal life and the forgiveness of sins.**
> **3. Help the believer grow in faith, love and knowledge.**

No doubt many books have done this and for those who prefer the usual type of book and who find them helpful and profitable – fair enough. These people are well catered for, but what about those people who find the traditional type of book unsuitable? We hope and pray that this book may help some of them.

The bulk of this book is in two parts

Section Two: **Questions with Aids to the Answers**

> For each chapter of John's gospel a number of questions are asked and in the right hand margin the helpful verses of that particular chapter, and occasionally helpful passages from elsewhere, are given.

Section Three	**Questions with Answers and Information**
	For each chapter of john's gospel the questions are repeated, but after each question there is an answer and sometimes various background or general information is given.
Section Four:	This draws together some of the main themes brought out in John's gospel.

Before commenting on "How to use this book", one very important point needs to be made.

> "Now the Bereans were of more noble character than the Thessalonians, for they received the message with great eagerness and examined the Scriptures every day to see if what Paul said was true. Many of the Jews believed..." (Acts 17:11, 12 NIV)

A read through the Acts will show that Paul had little success with the Jews. It was only those of Berea of whom it is said "many of the Jews believed", and so we ask, how did these Jews differ from the others?

1. "They received the message with great eagerness" is one aspect but note the second point:
2. *"and examined the Scriptures every day to see if what Paul said was true"*.

Dear readers please do the same with what is said in this book; and not only in this book, but in all you read relating to the Scriptures. Paul did not object when they checked on him, for, in doing so, they were described as being "of more noble character". This book is not infallible. It is an attempt to encourage people to find out truth for themselves and if the reader comes to a different answer . . . . !

In Luke 10:26 we see that the Lord's answer to a question was, "What is written in the Law? How do you read it?"

What if the Lord Jesus were to ask every person that question! Could you say what was written in Scripture and how you read it or understand it? Would you have to rely on the second-hand information, even though it may be right, or upon what you once heard someone say years ago, but you can't quite remember exactly what it was?

A teacher is important, especially in the beginning. The Ethiopian didn't understand what he was reading and said to Philip "How can I (understand) unless someone explains it to me?" (Acts 8:31 NIV). A teacher is important but his job should be getting people to find out for themselves, not, primarily, telling them what to believe.

2. HOW TO USE THIS BOOK

"How do I use this book?" the reader may ask. Well, that is up to you! It can be used in a variety of ways and this is why we hope it may be of use to different sorts of people. We give examples of how it can be used.

(1) If you have little knowledge of the Bible

- (a) Read John chapter 1 slowly and carefully.
- (b) Turn to Section Two of this book, "questions, hints and answers" then, without looking closely at the detailed answer provided use the hints, to attempt an answer to
  each question – either in your head or by writing it down.
- (c) Next, look at the answers to each question, as you do it, see if more information or a different answer has been given.
- (d) Work through all the questions on John chapter 1 and then the next day, or next week, read through John chapter 2.

(2) If you have read the Bible before:

- (a) Read John chapter 1 slowly and carefully.
- (b) Turn to Section Two, but without using the aids, attempt to answer all the questions – either in your head or by writing them down.

(c) If some question is unclear to you or you cannot think of an answer, then have a look at the hint for that particular question. It may be of some value.
(d) When all the questions on John Chapter 1 have been answered, compare your answers with the answers included following the hint verses and notice the extra information which may be given on certain points. Then the next day, or next week, read John chapter 2.

(3) *If you meet in a small group each week:*

You may care to give each of those who come a copy of the questions, or questions and hints, if they have not read the Bible very much. Alternatively, make up some questions of your own. Thus, may we suggest?

(a) At home each person can read John chapter 1 and attempt to answer all the questions given.
(b) At the meeting, after a reading aloud of John chapter 1, people can discuss what each has found out for each question. Within Section Two the detailed answers could be consulted to see if different light has been shed or more information given on each question as it arises. Alternatively, it may be best to discuss the whole of the chapter first and then to read the answers and information at the end.
(c) At the close of the meeting the questions on John chapter 2 could be given out.

(4) Other groups may care each week to discuss the contents of Section Three, "Questions, Answers and Information". At home each week, they could look at one chapter of John and the relevant comments made in this book and then meet to discuss what has been read.

(5) Some individuals may prefer to read straight through Section Three, "Questions, Answers and Information". These are asked to read each chapter of John's gospel before each set of questions is dealt with.

Thus, there are a variety of ways to use this book. Combinations of the above, or completely different ways, are also open to the reader. The above are just a few to give an idea. What is important is that the reader must find out for *himself* the best way of using this book in order that he may *grow in faith, love and knowledge of the Lord Jesus Christ.*

"But which Bible do I use?" is a common question asked. The New Testament references in this book have been taken from the *New International Version* and the Old Testament ones from the *King James Authorised Version*. The author himself prefers the AV but realises that for many its language is cumbersome and unclear. However, many of the modern versions are not translations but paraphrases. These have some value but contain many additions in their texts which are the ideas of those who worked on them.

If a Bible is to be purchased, may we suggest a copy of the *New International Version*, NIV. Also, a copy of the *King James Authorised Version*, AV would be of help. For those who have other versions and wish to use them, we think you will be able to do so without very much trouble (in fact the RV and RSV are valuable translations).

Throughout this book, references are given as follows:

2 Corinthians 4:10, 17 = 2 Corinthians 4 verses 10 and 17 only.
2 Corinthians 4:10-17 = 2 Corinthians 4 verses 10 to 17 inclusive.

3. WHY THIS BOOK WAS WRITTEN

> Amazing grace, how sweet the sound
> That saved a wretch like me.
> I once was lost, but now I'm found
> Was blind, but now I see.
>
> 'Twas grace that made this heart to fear
> And grace that fear relieved,
> How precious did that grace appear
> The hour I first believed.

That hymn was written by John Newton in the eighteenth century and found its way into the popular hit parades more than once in the early seventies. The music of the tune is light but good and the words are simple, yet sincere. Alas, not all who recorded it, not all who hum it, not all who whistle or try to sing it realize the depth of truth contained in the first verse alone. Thankfully, however, some do; and these have come to a knowledge and appreciation of God's "Amazing Grace" – grace that many find difficult to explain, for they know not the words needed to describe it and cannot find the words wanted to give thanks for it.

God's grace is intricately involved with the gift of His Son, the Lord Jesus Christ. God's grace is given to all who believe in, put their trust in, and have faith in the completed work of the Lord Jesus Christ. God's grace involves His forgetting all our frailties, failings and faults and accepting us just as we are. God's grace allows Him to do this for all who have faith in the Lord Jesus Christ's death and resurrection.

Now it is well known that many exercise faith in the completed work of the Lord Jesus. It is also well known that how and why they did so in the first place differs considerably from person to person. A very profitable time of fellowship can be spent in the company of other believers, hearing how each came first to believe, first to have faith in Christ. The different reasons, ways and answers will prove enlightening and, when we try to explain to those close to us exactly what happened and why we first trusted and believed, we may find it difficult to find the right words. However, we can all agree with the hymn ...

I was blind, but now I see.

The first act of faith in Christ, the initial belief a saved person has, is all important and will secure them forgiveness in the eyes of God. However He does not want people to stay in the position of, spiritually, new born babes. He wants people to grow and one purpose of the Christian life is to grow from faith to greater faith – "faith to faith". Now many realize that the initial faith and the way people come to first believe is very personal and individualistic. So it is that a great variety of meetings, different types of crusades, an assortment of tracts etc., etc., are used for this purpose; but isn't the growth in faith that follows just as individualistic? Having made the initial break-through with a variety of material, there is a tendency to give the same book to everyone or to send them all to *similar* meetings. This is understandable because, until we know a person well, we are not likely to be able to say exactly what is needed to help them grow or how best they can grow. But we do know that the way to grow spiritually is to come to a deeper knowledge of the Bible, the written Word of God, which makes known the Lord Jesus Christ, the Living Word.

This book is an attempt to present some of the different ways of reading and studying which enable people to grow and thus it hopes to meet the needs of a variety of people.

In this part we have tried to point out that it is important not only for the initial faith to be personal but also for the growing in faith to be personal. For this, the Berean attitude of seeing if a statement is true is essential and, if we find out for ourselves, there will be times when we disagree, but does that matter? What is important is that:

"All men will know that you are my disciples if you love *one another*".
(John 13:35)

SECTION TWO
Questions – with aids to the answers

QUESTIONS: JOHN CHAPTER 1 **AIDS**

1. The expression "the Word" is used four times in this passage. In which verses does it occur and to whom does it refer? — vs 1, 14. Compare vs 14,15 with vs 29, 30

2. Who was the Lord Jesus before He was born in Bethlehem and became the Son of God? — v 1

3. What part did the word of John 1:1 play in the creation? — vs 1-3. Compare with Genesis 1:1

4. The other main subject of this opening passage is the light. What is it and where can it be found? — v 4. See also John 5:21

5. Although life was obtainable in the Lord Jesus Christ and this life was the light of men, did all understand it? — v 5. See also John 3:19

6. Who came to bear witness of this light? — vs 6, 7

7. Why did this person bear witness of the light? — v 7

8. When the Creator came down into His creation, did it recognise Him and acknowledge Him? — v10

9. Did His own people receive Him as their Messiah and Saviour when He came to them? — v 11

10. The world did not recognise Him and His own did not receive Him but thankfully some did receive Him. What did He give to those who received Him?	vs 12, 13
11. Was His birth here on earth the beginning of His existence?	vs 1, 14
12. Is it possible that the great and mighty God of heaven became man and lived here on earth?	v 14
13. Can you explain John the Baptist's words in v 15?	vs 15, 30. Compare Luke 1, 2 with John 1:17
14. What was given through Moses?	v 17
15. What two things came into the world through Jesus Christ?	v 17
16. Has God in His essence as Spirit ever been seen by man?	v 18
17. Why did Christ come into the world as a man?	v 18
18. What questions did the priests and Levites ask John and what were his answers?	vs 19, 21, 21, 22, 22, 25
19. What description did John use of the Lord Jesus the "next day"?	vs 29, 36
20. Why did the Lord Jesus come into the world as the Lamb of God?	v 29
21. For what purpose did John baptise with water?	v 31
22. How was John to know the Son of God?	v 33
23. Who baptises with the Holy Spirit?	vs 32-34
24. Name one of John the Baptist's disciples who followed the Lord Jesus	vs 35, 40
25. Who was Andrew's brother?	v 40
26. What was the first thing Andrew did?	v 41
27. What did the Lord Jesus say to Simon?	v 42

28. What two words did the Lord Jesus say to Philip?	v 43
29. What was Nathanael's reply to Philip's statement?	v 46
30. What did the Lord Jesus first say to Nathanael?	v 47
31. What did the Lord Jesus reply to Nathanael's question?	v 48
32. What was Nathanael's testimony of the Lord Jesus?	v 49
33. Did Nathanael believe the Lord Jesus?	v 50

QUESTIONS: JOHN CHAPTER 2 **Aids**

34. What was the first miraculous sign performed by the Lord Jesus?	vs 1-10
35. What was the result of His performing this sign?	v 11
36. In the beginning of His ministry, what was the first thing the Lord Jesus did in Jerusalem?	vs 13-16
37. What Old Testament Scripture did this action prompt His disciples to remember?	v 17 and Psalm 69:9
38. What question did this action provoke the Jews to ask?	v 18
39. What was the Lord's reply to this question?	v 19
40. Did the Jews understand His reply?	v 20
41. Did the disciples understand His reply?	v 22
42. What happened in Jerusalem at the Passover feast?	v 23
43. Does the Lord Jesus know people? – i.e. does He know what they think and what they do?	vs 24, 25

Manual on the Gospel of John

QUESTIONS: JOHN CHAPTER 3

Aids

44. Who was Nicodemus?	v 1. See also John 7:47-52 and 19:38-42
45. What was his testimony of the Lord Jesus Christ?	v 2
46. At that time, how could one enter the kingdom?	vs 3, 5. Note John 1:12, 13
47. Did Nicodemus understand the Lord Jesus?	vs 4, 9
48. Should Nicodemus have understood?	v 10
49. What two important things did Nicodemus fail to do?	vs 11, 12
50. At the time that John wrote his gospel, had any man gone to heaven except the Son of Man – i.e. the Lord Jesus Christ?	v 13
51. What Old Testament miracle is foreshadowing Christ's death on the cross and the life obtainable to others from it?	v 14. Numbers 21:4-9
52. How can a person obtain resurrection which leads to eternal life?	vs 15-18. John 1:12, 13
53. What happens to those who do not believe Christ's words?	vs 16, 18
54. Who was to become greater and who was to become less important?	vs 29, 30
55. Who is above all?	v 31. See also John 1:1, 14
56. Who has eternal life?	v 36
57. What happens to those who are condemned – i.e. those who reject the Lord Jesus?	vs 16, 18, and 36

QUESTIONS: JOHN CHAPTER 4

58. Was the Lord Jesus baptising people Himself?	vs 1, 2
59. Why did the Lord Jesus leave Judea?	vs 1-3
60. The Lord Jesus left Judea and went back to Galilee. Which country did He pass through and in which town did He stop?	vs 4, 5
61. Why was the woman surprised that the Lord Jesus asked her for a drink?	v 9
62. What was the gift of God the Lord Jesus referred to?	vs 10, 14 see also John 6:35
63. What type of water did the Lord Jesus offer the woman and how does it differ from ordinary water?	vs 13, 14. See also John 6:35
64. Did the Samaritan woman understand what this water was?	v 15
65. In what special way must God be worshipped?	vs 20-24
66. Who did the Lord Jesus say He was?	vs 25, 26
67. What three descriptions did the Samaritan woman use of the Lord Jesus?	vs 9,19,29. Note also verse 42
68. What did the Lord Jesus say His food was?	v 34
69. For what is the crop harvested?	v 36. Note also vs 35-38
70. Why did the Samaritans first believe?	v 39. Note also vs 41, 42
71. After knowing the Lord Jesus, who did the men of Samaria believe Him to be?	v 42
72. What was the Lord's second miracle in Galilee?	v 46-54
73. What was the result of that miracle?	v 53

QUESTIONS: JOHN CHAPTER 5   Aids

74. What was the man's reply to the Lord's question?	v 7
75. What was the Lord's next miraculous sign?	vs 5-15
76. Why did the Jews in Jerusalem get annoyed with the Lord Jesus and want to persecute Him?	v 16
77. Why did they want to kill Him?	vs 17, 18
78. Why has all judgment been given to the Son?	vs 22, 23
79. How does a person cross from death to life?	vs 21, 24
80. What do verses 19 to 30 say about resurrection?	vs 21, 25, 28, 29
81. Why is the Lord Jesus Christ's judgment just?	vs 22, 30
82. How could the Jews know that the Father has sent the Son into the world?	v 36
83. Can the Bible give a person eternal life?	v 39
84. Can the Bible help a person find how to obtain eternal life?	vs 39, 40
85. Should a believer feel satisfied with human praise?	vs 41-44
86. Did all the Jews believe what Moses wrote?	vs 45-47.

QUESTIONS: JOHN CHAPTER 6   Aids

87. Did the Gentiles observe the Passover?	v 4
88. Was there enough food for the 5,000?	v 9-13
89. What did this miraculous sign provoke the people to say?	v 14

Manual on the Gospel of John

90. What did the people want to do with the Lord Jesus?	v 15
91. Did the Jews who followed the Lord Jesus to the other side of the lake have their priorities right?	v 15, 26, 27
92. What is the Work of God?	v 29
93. Was it a mark of unbelief for the Jews to ask for a sign?	v 30, 31
94. What is the true bread of heaven?	vs 32, 33
95. When do these people start their eternal life?	v 39, 40, 44
96. Who is the only one to have seen the Father?	v 46. Note also John 5:37 and 1:18
97. Which previous verse in John's Gospel is like verse 47?	v 3:16 and others
98. What does the Lord Jesus mean when He uses the figure "eat of the bread"?	v 51. Please compare verses 40, 47, 48 with verses 53, 54
99. What is the difference between this true bread of heaven and the manna of the Old Testament?	v 58
100. What was really wrong with this people?	v 64
101. What was Peter's confession?	v 68, 69

QUESTIONS: JOHN CHAPTER 7	**Aids**
102. Why did the Lord Jesus stay away from Judea?	v 1
103. Did His own brothers believe in Him?	vs 3-5
104. Why were the Jews amazed?	v 15. Note also verses 16-19
105. Did they know where the Christ was to come from?	v 27
106. Why did the crowd try to seize the Lord Jesus?	v 28-30

107. Why were they unable to do so?	v 30
108. Which verses help to explain what the Lord Jesus said to the Samaritan woman in John chapter 4?	Compare v 4:14 with vs 7:37-39
109. What were the people saying about the Lord Jesus?	vs 40, 41, 42
110. Had any of the Pharisees put their trust in Him?	v 50, 51. Compare 3:1 with 7:50 and 19:39

QUESTIONS: JOHN CHAPTER 8   Aids

111. Is there a record that the Lord Jesus ever wrote anything?	vs 6, 8
112. What did the Lord Jesus say to the woman who was taken in sin?	v 11
113. What sort of Judge is the Lord Jesus?	vs 15, 16. See also 5:22, 30
114. How can a person not die in their sins?	v 24
115. What is verse 28 referring to?	v 28
116. Please read verses 12-29 again very carefully. What happened to people who heard the Lord Jesus speak?	v 30
117. What are we told about everyone who sins?	v 34
118. How can someone be set free from slavery?	vs 35, 36. Note also verse 31, 32
119. Who did the Jews claim was their father?	vs 39, 41
120. Why were their claims not true?	vs 40, 41, 42
121. Who did the Lord Jesus say was their father?	v 44
122. Who is the father of lies?	v 44
123. Was the Lord Jesus guilty of sin?	v 46. Also 1 Peter 2:22.
124. Did Abraham see the Lord's day?	v 56. Also Hebrews 11

Manual on the Gospel of John

125. Why did the Jews want to stone the Lord Jesus?	vs 58, 59

QUESTIONS: JOHN CHAPTER 9 — Aids

126. Why was the man born blind?	vs 2, 3
127. How did the Lord Jesus heal the blind man?	vs 6, 7
128. The man was asked several questions about how he received his sight. What was his answer on each occasion?	v 10
129. Did the Pharisees listen to reason?	vs 28, 29, 34
130. What is worse than physical blindness?	vs 35-41

QUESTIONS: JOHN CHAPTER 10 — Aids

131. How do thieves and robbers get into the sheep pen?	v 1
132. Will sheep follow these strangers?	vs 3-5
133. Did the people understand the figure of speech used by the Lord Jesus?	v 6
134. Do you understand this figure of speech?	vs 1-18
135. What will the good shepherd do for his sheep?	v 11
136. Could anyone lay down his life for the sheep?	vs 11-13
137. What does the Lord Jesus Christ have to say about His death?	vs 17, 18
138. Did the Jews accept the Lord's prediction of His resurrection?	vs 19-21
139. Did the Gentiles keep the Feast of Dedication?	vs 22-24
140. Did the Lord Jesus plainly admit that He was the Christ?	vs 24, 25. Also verses 4:26 and 9:35-37

Manual on the Gospel of John

141. What does the Lord Jesus, the Good Shepherd, do for His sheep?	v 28
142. What does the Lord Jesus mean by the statement "I and the Father are one"?	vs 30-33
143. Why did the Jews try and seize the Lord Jesus?	vs 34-39
144. Did John the Baptist do any miraculous signs?	v 41

QUESTIONS: JOHN CHAPTER 11   Aids

145. When the Lord Jesus heard that Lazarus was sick, did He go immediately to help him?	v 6
146. What word does the Lord Jesus use to describe death?	vs 11-14
147. How long was Lazarus in the grave?	v 17
148. What did Martha say to the Lord Jesus?	vs 21, 22
149. Did Martha believe she would see her brother again?	vs 23, 24
150. What happens to believers who are dead?	vs 24-26
151. "Jesus wept" is the shortest verse in the Bible. Why did He weep"?	vs 17-44
152. What did the Lord Jesus say to Lazarus and what happened?	vs 43, 44
153. What was the result of this miraculous sign?	v 45
154. What were the Pharisees concerned about?	v 48
155. What did Caiaphas say would happen to the Lord Jesus?	vs 49-52

QUESTIONS: JOHN CHAPTER 12   Aids

156. What did Mary do for the Lord Jesus?	v 3
157. Was Judas Iscariot's objection well motivated?	vs 4-6
158. Why did the Jews want to kill Lazarus?	vs 10, 11 and also 17-19
159. What Old Testament Scripture did the Lord Jesus fulfil on His entry into Jerusalem?	v 15. Zechariah 9:9
160. Did the disciples realise, at that time, that such prophecies were being fulfilled?	v 16
161. Who else were among the Jews who went up to the feast?	v 20
163. What did the Lord Jesus say about those who love and hate life?	v 25. Note also Matthew 16:24-28
164. Did the Lord Jesus want to be saved from His hour of death?	v 27
165. Did the Lord Jesus know what kind of death He was to suffer?	vs 32, 33
166. Did the crowd think that the Christ would remain forever?	v 34
167. How does one become a son of light?	v 36. Also 1:6-9; 8:12; 9:5
168. What prophet of the Old Testament predicted the attitude of the Jewish leaders to the Lord Jesus?	v 38 – Isaiah 53:1 v 40 – Isaiah 6:9, 10
169. Why had the prophet predicted these things?	v 41. Compare 8:56
170. What difficulties did those leaders who wanted to confess their faith in the Lord Jesus have put in front of them?	vs 42, 43
171. Is it possible to have real belief in the Lord Jesus without a belief in the Father?	v 44

172. Does it matter that no one has seen God in His essence as Spirit?	vs 44, 45
173. What was the purpose of the Lord Jesus Christ's first coming?	v 46
174. Did He come to judge the world?	v 47
175. What happens to those who reject the Lord Jesus?	v 48

QUESTIONS: JOHN CHAPTER 13 — Aids

176. When did the events of this chapter take place?	v 1
177. Who promoted Judas Iscariot to betray the Lord Jesus?	v 2
178. Was the Lord Jesus above doing the work of a slave or servant?	vs 4, 5. Note also verses 14-17
179. Was Peter impetuous?	vs 6-9 and 21-25. Matthew 16:13-23; 14:22-36. John 13:31-38
180. What should the Lord Jesus be called by those who follow Him?	vs 13, 14
181. Is a servant greater than his master?	v 16. Note vs 1-14
182. Which Old Testament Scripture is next fulfilled?	v 18. Psalm 41:9
183. What is the purpose of predicting events?	v 19. Note John 14:29
184. Did the disciples, at that time, realise what Judas was about to do?	vs 28, 29
185. When did Satan enter Judas?	v 27
186. When did Judas leave the Lord Jesus and the eleven?	vs 27, 30
187. Who is to be glorified?	vs 31, 32
188. What new commandment was given to the disciples?	v 34. Read 1 Corinthians 13
189. How were people to know His disciples?	v 35

Manual on the Gospel of John

190. Will the Lord Jesus come back for the disciples?	v 3

QUESTIONS: JOHN CHAPTER 14 — Aids

191. What was the way to the place the Lord Jesus is talking about?	v 6. John 10:1-21
192. How does one get to see the Father?	vs 7-15. Note verses 7 and 9. Also verses 10, 11
193. Would the disciples do greater things than the Lord Jesus?	v 12. See Acts 5:15; 19:12
194. What does verse 14 mean?	v 14. Matt. 21:22; Mark 11:24; Luke 22:42; 1 John 5:14, 16
195. Who was to be within the disciples?	vs 17, 21
196. How can one show one's love for the Lord Jesus?	vs 21, 23. Note verse 15
197. What was the Counsellor, the Holy Spirit, to do for the disciples?	v 26
198. Who is the "Prince of this World" and does he have any effect on the Lord Jesus?	v 30

QUESTIONS: JOHN CHAPTER 15 — Aids

199. Who is the vine and who is the gardener	vs 1, 5
200. Why should we be careful to abide in Christ?	vs 1-8. Note verses 4, 5
201. What is the greatest love a person can have?	v 13. Note Romans 5:7-10
202. Did the disciples choose the Lord Jesus?	v 16
203. Why does the world hate believers in the Lord Jesus?	vs 18-20.
204. Did the Jews have any excuse for their sin?	vs 22-24
205. Why did the world hate the Lord Jesus?	vs 22-25

206. What will the Holy Spirit, the Spirit of truth, do?	v 26. Also John 14:26
207. Who else must testify?	v 27
208. Why must these testify?	v 27

QUESTIONS: JOHN CHAPTER 16   Aids

209. What is to happen to the disciples?	vs 2, 3
210. Why was it necessary for the Lord Jesus to go away?	v 7
211. What was to be the work of the Counsellor, the Holy Spirit, when He came?	vs 8-11
212. Of whom was the Spirit of truth to speak?	vs 13-15. Also John 15:26
213. Did the disciples understand what the Lord Jesus was referring to in verse 16?	vs 16-18
214. What is the Lord Jesus referring to in verse 20?	vs 20, 22
215. When will the disciples be able to ask anything in the Lord's name	vs 23, 26. Also note John 14:20
216. Why did the Father love them?	v 27. Compare with John 3:16
217. Did the disciples understand the Lord Jesus when He no longer used figures of speech?	vs 29, 30
218. Did they believe He came from God?	v 30
219. Where could the disciples find peace and why?	v 33. Also John 14:27

QUESTIONS: JOHN CHAPTER 17   Aids

220. What is life eternal?	v 3
221. Read carefully the Lord's prayer for His disciples.	vs 6-19
222. Did the disciples accept the word of the Lord Jesus?	vs 7, 8

223. Who is the child of hell (literally "son of perdition")?	v 12. John 13:2, 18, 27
224. Did He want His disciples taken out of this world?	v 15
225. Read carefully the Lord's prayer for all believers.	vs 20-26
226. Why did the Lord Jesus want all believers to be a complete unity?	v 23
227. How do we get to know the Father?	vs 25, 26
228. What happened to the soldiers and the officers when the Lord Jesus gave His title "I AM"?	vs 4-6
229. What did Peter do?	v 10. Luke 9:2-5, Luke 22:35-38

QUESTIONS: JOHN CHAPTER 18   **Aids**

230. Did the Lord Jesus resist arrest?	vs 7-11. Compare with 7:30 and 8:20
231. What did the Lord Jesus mean when He said, "Shall I not drink the cup the Father has given me?"?	v 11 and John 12:27
232. When had Caiaphas advised the Jews that it would be best if one man died for the people?	v 14. Compare with 11:49, 50
233. What does the Lord Jesus say about His teaching?	v 20
234. Did Peter prove the Lord Jesus right?	v 17-27. Compare with John 13:38
235. Why did the Jews not judge the Lord Jesus themselves?	v 31
236. Was the Lord's kingdom of this world?	v 36
237. Did the Lord Jesus answer the question "Are you the king of the Jews?"?	vs 33-37
238. What was Pilate's opinion after he had examined the Lord Jesus?	v 38
239. Did the people want the Lord Jesus to be freed?	v 40

QUESTIONS: JOHN CHAPTER 19   Aids

240. How was the Lord Jesus treated by the soldiers?	vs 1-3
241. Did Pilate find the Lord Jesus guilty of anything at all?	vs 4-6. Also 18:38
242. Was Pilate to bear the responsibility of the Lord's death?	vs 1-16 and note verse 11
243. What seven questions did Pilate ask the Lord Jesus? (Four are in chapter 18).	See 18:33, 35, 37, 38; 19:9, 10, 10
244. Where was the Lord Jesus to be executed?	v 17
245. What title did Pilate write on the cross?	v 19
246. What prophecy was next fulfilled?	v 24 – Psalm 22:18, verse 29 – Psalm 69:21
247. What women were present at the scene?	v 25
248. Who was the disciple the Lord Jesus loved and what did He ask him to do?	vs 26, 27. John 21:20, 21
249. What were the last words uttered by the Lord Jesus on the cross?	vs 17-30, Matthew 27:33-50; Mark 15:22-39; Luke 23:33-47
250. When did the Lord Jesus die on the cross?	vs 14, 31. Matthew 27:62, Mark 15:42, Luke 23:54
251. Why did the soldiers not break His legs?	vs 31-37. Note verse 33. Compare verse 36 with Psalm 34:20, 37 with Zechariah 12:10
252. Who helped Joseph of Arimathea with the body of the Lord Jesus?	v 39

QUESTIONS: JOHN CHAPTER 20   Aids

253. What did Mary say when she found the tomb empty?	v 2
254. What did the Lord Jesus have to do?	vs 6-9. Note verse 9
255. Did the other disciple see and believe?	v 8

256. What was Mary's reply to the angel?	v 13
257. What was Mary's reply to the Lord Jesus?	vs 15, 16
258. Could the disciples forgive sins?	vs 22, 23
259. What was Thomas' comment when the others told him that they had seen the Lord Jesus?	vs 25
260. What was Thomas' statement when he himself saw the Lord Jesus?	v 28
261. What was the reply the Lord Jesus made to that statement?	v 29
262. Why did John write his gospel?	vs 30, 31

QUESTIONS: JOHN CHAPTER 21   Aids

263. Did they realise it was the Lord Jesus talking to them?	v 4
264. Who said to Peter "It is the Lord"?	v 7
265. Did the disciples know it was the Lord Jesus?	v 12
266. How many times had the Lord Jesus appeared to His disciples after His death?	v 14
267. What three questions did the Lord Jesus ask Peter?	vs 15-17
268. What four instructions did He give Peter	vs 15, 16, 17, 1
271. Did the Lord Jesus do many other things?	v 25. Also John 20:30

Manual on the Gospel of John

SECTION THREE
Questions – Answers and Information on John's Gospel

ANSWERS WITH QUESTIONS: CHAPTER 1

1. The expression "the Word" is used four times in this passage. In which verses does it occur and to whom does it refer?

    A. Three times in 1:1 and once in 1:14.

In verse 1 we are told that "the Word was God".

In verse 14 we are told that "the Word became flesh".

By comparing verses 14, 15, i.e. –

"*The Word became flesh* and lived for a while among us. We have seen his glory, the glory of the one and only son, who came from the Father, full of grace and truth. John testifies concerning him. He cries out, saying '*This was he* of whom I said, "*He who comes after me has surpassed me because he was before me*"'. With verses 29, 30, i.e. –

"The next day John saw *Jesus* coming toward him and said, 'Look, the Lamb of God, who takes away the sin of the world! *This is the one I meant* when I said, "*A man who comes after me has surpassed me because he was before me*"'.

We see "the Word" is the Lord Jesus Christ.

2. Who was the Lord Jesus before He was born in Bethlehem and became the Son of God?

    A. In verse 1 we read "the Word was God".
Now "the Word" refers to the Lord Jesus Christ. Thus, before He was born in Bethlehem and became the Son of God, He was the Word. He was God.

3. What part did the word of John 1:1 play in the creation?

    A. Please note the following:
    1:1 "In the *beginning* was the Word".
        "The Word was God".
    1:2 "He was with God in the *beginning*".
    1:3 "Through him all things were made; without him nothing was made that has been made".

Compare these statements with the opening words of the Bible in Genesis 1:1

"In the *beginning* God created the heavens and the earth".

Thus we see that "the Word" existed in the *beginning* as did God, and the creation and making of all things is attributed to them both. Thus, they are the same being.

4. The other main subject of this opening passage is the light. What is it and where can it be found?

    A. Here we see that the light was the life which is found in the Lord Jesus. In verse 4 we read "In him was life and the life was the light of men". Please read John 5:21 where it states "For just as the Father raises the dead and gives them life, even so the son gives life to whom he is pleased to give it".

Thus the Lord Jesus is able to give life, eternal life after a resurrection, to whom He pleases – and that includes you and me. How to obtain this life we shall soon find out.

5. Although life was obtainable in the Lord Jesus Christ and this life was the light of men, did all understand it?

    A. Unfortunately, no. In verse 5 we read, "The light shines in the darkness, but the darkness has not understood it."

The reader may think that darkness refers to ignorance and superstition etc. However, it is obvious that those in darkness could not understand the light, i.e. they could not understand the life which is obtainable in the Lord Jesus.

To understand what is meant by darkness, consider the following examples:

1) In verse 11 it states that His own people rejected Him, and this was after He had ministered to them for 3 ½ years.
2) In John 3:19 we read, "Light has come into the world, but men loved darkness instead of light because their deeds were evil. Everyone who does evil hates the light, and will not come into the light for fear that his deeds will be exposed.

Here is one reason why darkness has not understood light. Here we see why some fail to appreciate the Lord Jesus.

6. Who came to bear witness of this light?

    A. From verses 6 and 7 we see it is John.

    He is usually referred to as John the Baptist and this serves not to confuse him with John the Apostle who wrote this gospel.

7. Why did this person bear witness of the light?

    A. From verse 7 we see the reason was "… that through him all men might believe". We shall find out later what we are to believe in and why it is so important.

8. When the Creator came down into His creation, did it recognise Him and acknowledge Him?

    A. No – read verse 10.

9. Did His own people receive Him as their Messiah and Saviour when He came to them?

A. No – read verse 11.

10. The world did not recognise Him and His own did not receive Him but thankfully some did receive Him. What did He give to those who received Him?

A. We read in verses 12 and 13.

> "Yet to all who did receive him, to those who believed in his name, he gave the right to become children of God — children born not of natural descent, nor of human decision or a husband's will, but born of God".

Thus, those who received Him, those who believed in His name, He gave them the right to become children of God, children born of God. With this privilege goes another which we shall soon see.

11. Was His birth here on earth the beginning of His existence?

A. No - Verse 1 states "In the beginning was the Word" and this "beginning" refers to a time before the heavens and earth were created; infinity in the past, if you like. Verse 14 then tells us that "The Word became flesh" and this refers to the start of His earthly life, not the beginning of His existence.

12. Is it possible that the great and mighty God of heaven became man and lived here on earth?

A. Yes – read verse 14.

13. Can you explain John the Baptist's words in verse 15?

A. John's words are "He who comes after me has surpassed me because he was before me". John uses this expression again in verse 30.

The person to whom John is referring is the Lord Jesus Christ, "the Word". Now, "the Word" existed in the beginning and thus before John ever existed. However, "the Word became flesh" and

His earthly life among us started as a baby in Bethlehem. This miraculous birth took place after the birth of John the Baptist. (Read Luke Chapters 1 and 2)

14. What was given through Moses?
   A. The law – verse 17.

15. What two things came into the world through Jesus Christ?
   A. From verse 17 we see they are "grace" and "truth".

16. Has God in His essence as Spirit ever been seen by man?
   A. No – read verse 18.

17. Why did Christ come into the world as a man?
   A. There are many reasons but one is given in verse 18 – i.e. to make God known. Many religions teach of man's striving to contact the infinite God and some agnostics say that it is impossible for man to know if God exists, because it is beyond man's capacity to contact Him. This is true but it is *not* beyond the capability of the infinite God to contact man. If it were, He would cease to be the infinite God.

18. What questions did the priests and Levites ask John and what were his answers?
   Q v 19 "… Levites to ask him who he was".
   A v 20 "I am not the Christ".
   Q v 21 "Then who are you? Are you Elijah?"
   A v 21 "I am not".
   Q v 21 "Are you the prophet?"
   A v 21 "No".
   Q v 22 "Who are you … What do you say about yourself?"
   A v 23 "I am the voice of one calling in the desert, 'Make straight the way of the Lord'".
   Q v 25 "When then do you baptise if you are not the Christ, nor Elijah nor the Prophet?"

A vs 26, 27 Read these verses and note John's reply. He does not say why he baptises with water at this point. He does so later on; see verse 31.

19. What description did John use of the Lord Jesus the "next day"?
A. From verse 29 we see John called the Lord Jesus "the Lamb of God". This expression is used again in verse 36.

20. Why did the Lord Jesus come into the world as the Lamb of God?
A. Verse 29 explains it was to "take away the sin of the world".

This verse may be difficult to understand today. However, John the Baptist was talking to those who had been brought up in the ways of the Old Testament where, if a person sinned, forgiveness was obtained if some animal, such as a lamb, was taken to the priests for them to sacrifice and place the blood on the altar. The purpose of this was to teach the people symbolically that one day there would have to be a real sacrifice for sin, because as Romans 6:23 states, "the wages of sin is death, but the gift of God is eternal life through Christ Jesus our Lord". Thus God came into the world in the person of the Lord Jesus Christ and took upon Himself a human body and so made the complete sacrifice on the cross. This enables the sins of all believers in Christ, from all ages, to be forgiven. Thus, there is no need for animal sacrifice today and its real value in the Old Testament was to teach the people what would happen one day.

As we look back at Christ's death and accept it by faith as the sacrifice for our sins, so those in Old Testament times looked ahead to His death and by faith also they could accept it as the sacrifice for their sins. Thus, forgiveness is obtainable by all believers of all times through their faith in what God did once just over 2000 years ago.

21. For what purpose did John baptise with water?
A. Read verse 31 very carefully and note the reason.

22. How was John to know the Son of God?
   A. Read verse 33.

23. Who baptises with the Holy Spirit?
   A. Read verses 32-34 and note the person talked about is here called "The Son of God". Note the different titles used of Him so far:
   (a) Verse 34 "The Son of God"
   (b) Verse 30 and 15 "A man who comes after me has surpassed me because he was before me".
   (c) Verse 29 "The lamb of God, who takes away the sin of the world".
   (d) Verse 18 "God the only Son"
   (e) Verse 17 "Jesus Christ"
   (f) Verse 14 and 1 "The Word".

   There may also be others. The titles of the Lord Jesus are many and varied and they endeavour to show different aspects of His character and different aspects of the work He came to accomplish.

24. Name one of John the Baptist's disciples who followed the Lord Jesus.
   A. From verse 35 we see that there were two of John's disciples who followed the Lord Jesus. One is named in verse 40 – i.e. Andrew. The other is not named and it could be John, the writer of the Gospel, for nowhere in this book does he mention himself by name.

25. Who was Andrew's brother?
   A. Simon Peter – see verse 40.

26. What was the first thing Andrew did?
   A. See verse 41 and note Andrew uses another title of the Lord Jesus.

27. What did the Lord Jesus say to Simon?

      A. See verse 42.

28. What two words did the Lord Jesus say to Philip?
      A. "Follow me". See verse 43.

29. What was Nathanael's reply to Philip's statement?
      A. "Nazareth! Can anything good come from there?" See verse 46.

30. What did the Lord Jesus first say to Nathanael?
      A. "Here is an Israelite, in whom there is nothing false". See verse 47.

31. What did the Lord Jesus reply to Nathanael's question?
      A. "I saw you while you were still under the fig tree before Philip called you". Verse 48.

32. What was Nathanael's testimony of the Lord Jesus?
      A. "Rabbi, you are the Son of God; you are the King of Israel" – Verse 49.
      Note how Nathanael changed his mind about things from Nazareth.

33. Did Nathanael believe the Lord Jesus?
      A. From the Lord's reply in verse 50 it is clear that Nathanael believed Him. Note how the Lord Jesus pointed out that Nathanael first believed little things and was thus going to see greater things.

ANSWERS WITH QUESTIONS: CHAPTER 2

34. What was the first miraculous sign performed by the Lord Jesus?
      A. Read verses 1-10.
      For those who find the expression 'my time has not yet come' perplexing, we would point out that it occurs several times in John's Gospel and is discussed later.

35. What was the result of His performing this sign?
> **A.** Verse 11.
> "He thus revealed his glory, and his disciples put their *faith* in him".

36. In the beginning of His ministry, what was the first thing the Lord Jesus did in Jerusalem?
> **A.** Read verses 13-16.
> Note that the disciples put their faith in Him and not in the religious establishment of their day, which had obviously got its priorities wrong. There is a lesson for us to learn from this.

37. What Old Testament Scripture did this action prompt His disciples to remember?
> **A.** Read verse 17.
> "Zeal for your house will consume me". This is a quotation from Psalm 69:9.

38. What question did this action provoke the Jews to ask?
Verse 18.
> **A.** "What miraculous sign can you show us to prove your authority to do all this?"

39. What was the Lord's reply to this question?
> **A.** Verse 19.
> The sign was, "Destroy this temple, and I will raise it again in three days".

40. Did the Jews understand His reply?
> **A.** From verse 20 they evidently did not, but verse 21 makes the Lord's meaning clear.

41. Did the disciples understand His reply?
Read verse 22.
> **A.** After the Lord Jesus' resurrection from the dead, not only did they understand, but, because He had foretold what would happen to Him and what He would do three or more years before

Manual on the Gospel of John

it happened, "They *believed* the Scripture and the words that Jesus had spoken".

It is important to believe and have spiritual understanding. However, a person can have intellectual understanding and not believe. Mere intellectual appreciation of the Scriptures does not, of itself, give spiritual understanding.

42. What happened in Jerusalem at the Passover feast?
    A. Verse 23.
    "Many people saw the miraculous sign he was doing and *trusted* in his name".

43. Does the Lord Jesus know people? – i.e. does He know what they think and what they do?
    A. Verse 24 "… He knew all men".
    Verse 25 "… He knew what was in a man".

Even today, He still knows all men and He knows what is in them.

ANSWERS WITH QUESTIONS: CHAPTER 3

44. Who was Nicodemus?
    A. From verse 1 we see that he was a Pharisee and a member of the Jewish ruling council which is called the Sanhedrin.

In what follows notice Nicodemus' shaky start, but he appears again in John 7:50 and note John 19:38-42. Here we see that Nicodemus helped with the crucified body of Christ. Thus we can learn a lesson from this person. He found things difficult and did not fully understand in the beginning, yet he remained faithful.

45. What was his testimony of the Lord Jesus Christ?
    Read verse 2.

46. At that time, how could one enter the kingdom?

A. Verse 3.

"...Unless a man is born again, he cannot see the kingdom of God". The expression "born again" can be translated "born from above" and shows that some action is needed from the One who is above – this action being to impart spiritual life.

In John 1:12, 13 we have read, "Yet to all who received him, to those who believed in his name, he gave the right to become the Children of God – children born not of natural descent, nor of human decision or a husband's will, but born of God".

To be "born again", "born from above", "born of God" – i.e. to become a child of God – a person needed to receive the Lord Jesus Christ and to "believe in his name".

Verse 5. "... unless a man is born of water and the Spirit, he cannot enter the Kingdom of God". The reader may think that water baptism is being referred to here, but don't forget that this section is a fuller explanation of verse 3. Thus verse 5 is explaining in greater detail the expression "born again" which we have seen is totally dependent upon the response of a person to the Lord Jesus – i.e. a person's faith, belief etc.

Two views will be put and we will leave the reader to decide for himself:

(a) The expression "born of water and the Spirit" is a figure of speech where one thing and not two is meant. Thus it means "born of Spiritual water". This would show Nicodemus that it was nothing to do with an earthly birth, which was his idea in verse 4, and it should have helped him to understand the meaning of "born again" or "born from above", as it points out the spiritual side. We use a similar figure of speech in everyday language in this age. For example, at the tea table we may ask someone to "pass the *bread and butter*" but what we are asking for is *buttered bread* and not two separate items.

(b) Nicodemus was a Pharisee and had probably been baptised by John. We know from Matthew 3:7-11 that John did baptise some Pharisees. The Pharisees had a great love for ceremony and thus, having undergone John's baptism, Nicodemus thought that nothing else was needed. In this passage the Lord Jesus points out to him the futility of trusting in earthly things, see verse 6, and thus the futility of water baptism, if it were not followed by the thing that really mattered – i.e. a belief in the Lord Jesus which would produce the child of God. Nicodemus had been baptised in water but now he *had* to be born of the Spirit, i.e. born again, by receiving the Lord Jesus. Thus "unless a man is born of water *AND* THE SPIRIT (which is the essential part) he cannot enter the kingdom of God".

47. Did Nicodemus understand the Lord Jesus?

A. From verse 4 it is clear that Nicodemus had obviously misunderstood and had confused the new birth from above with a second earthly birth. So the Lord Jesus answers him in more detail – read verses 5-8; yet from verse 9 it is clear that Nicodemus still doesn't understand.

48. Should Nicodemus have understood?

A. Yes, because he was a teacher of Israel.

49. What two important things did Nicodemus fail to do?

A. Verse 11 "You people do not accept our testimony".
Verse 12 "I have spoken to you of earthly things and you do *not* believe; how then will you believe if I speak of heavenly things?"

We can see that there are many today who do not accept the testimony of our Lord Jesus and who show great reluctance to believe anything.

50. At the time that John wrote his gospel, had any man gone to heaven except the Son of Man – i.e. the Lord Jesus Christ?

A. From verse 13 the answer is 'No'.

What we are given is a promise of eternal life to be commenced on the day of resurrection – e.g. we have already read John 5:21, "For just as the Father raises the dead and gives them life, even so the Son gives life to whom he is pleased to give it".

51. What Old Testament miracle is foreshadowing Christ's death on the cross and the life obtainable to others from it?

A. Read verse 14.

Details can be obtained from the fourth book of the Old Testament, Numbers 21:4-9.

52. How can a person obtain resurrection which leads to eternal life?

A. Verse 15 "… everyone who believes may have eternal life in him".

Verse 16 "For God so loved the world that he gave his one and only Son, that whoever believes in him shall not perish but have everlasting life".

Verse 17 "For God did not send his Son into the world to condemn the world, but to save the world through him".

Verse 18 "Whoever believes in him is not condemned".

Please note two things. First, these verses can only refer to those who have heard of the Lord Jesus Christ. Those who have not heard cannot come under this criterion. They come under another part of God's plan which is dealt with elsewhere in the Bible and perhaps we shall look at it one day.

Secondly, note the emphasis upon" belief" in Christ. This word and others like it –i.e. faith and trust – have occurred a number of times already in the opening pages of this Gospel and it is the criterion God uses for viewing people. Nothing else is required. The reader may think baptism is necessary but we see no reference is made to this in these verses which speak of the promise of eternal life. Also John gives the reason for baptising in Christ in John 1:31, "The reason I came baptising with water was that he (the Lord Jesus) might be revealed to *Israel*".

53. What happens to those who do not believe Christ's words?

A. From verse 16 it is clear that those who believe in Christ shall not perish and thus those who do not believe in Him shall perish. This is the meaning of verse 18 which shows that those who do not believe in Christ are condemned to perishing.

54. Who was to become greater and who was to become less important?
A. Verse 30.
The Lord Jesus is to become greater; John the Baptist is to become less important.

55. Who is above all?

A. "The Word was God", 1:1
"The Word became flesh", 1:14
"The one who comes from above is above all", 3:31

It is the Lord Jesus Christ who is above all.

56. Who has eternal life?
A. Verse 36. "Whoever puts his faith in the Son has eternal life".

57. What happens to those who are condemned – i.e. those who reject the Lord Jesus?

A. Verse 36.
"...whoever rejects the Son will not see that life – i.e. eternal life. The reader may think that verse 18 says that horrible things happen to those who are condemned but from verse 36 we see that the condemnation, the judgment is that they are not given eternal life, they perish. From the other parts of the Bible, we see that all will be raised from the dead to give account of themselves before God. Then some will experience the second death. Thus those who have belief in the Lord Jesus will have eternal life and those who do not believe will not have eternal life.

ANSWERS WITH QUESTIONS: CHAPTER 4

58. Was the Lord Jesus baptising people Himself?
    A. No – verses 1 and 2.

59. Why did the Lord Jesus leave Judea?
    A. Probably because of possible repercussions over the Pharisees' reports that the Lord Jesus was having a greater impact than John the Baptist. The Pharisees tolerated John but the Lord Jesus was going to cause them much more concern.

60. The Lord Jesus left Judea and went back to Galilee. Which country did He pass through and in which town did He stop?
    A. From verses 4 and 5 we see that to go from Judea to Galilee the Lord Jesus had to pass through the region known as Samaria and He stopped in the town of Sychar. Please see the map which follows and which shows the movements of people up to this point.

61. Why was the woman surprised that the Lord Jesus asked her for a drink?
    A. To a Jew there would be a double prejudice in this encounter; one, on the grounds of her sex, the other because of

her race. Verse 9 states that Jews did not associate with Samaritans; yet in verse 12 we see that they claimed Jacob as a forefather. Thus, the Samaritans had also descended from Abraham who was the father of Isaac, who was the father of Jacob. Why was there trouble between the Jews and the Samaritans?

After King Solomon's death about 880 B.C. the Jewish nation split in two. The northern Kingdom was based at the town of Samaria and occupied the region known as Samaria and the southern kingdom made its headquarters in Jerusalem, which had been the headquarters of the united nation in David's and Solomon's time.

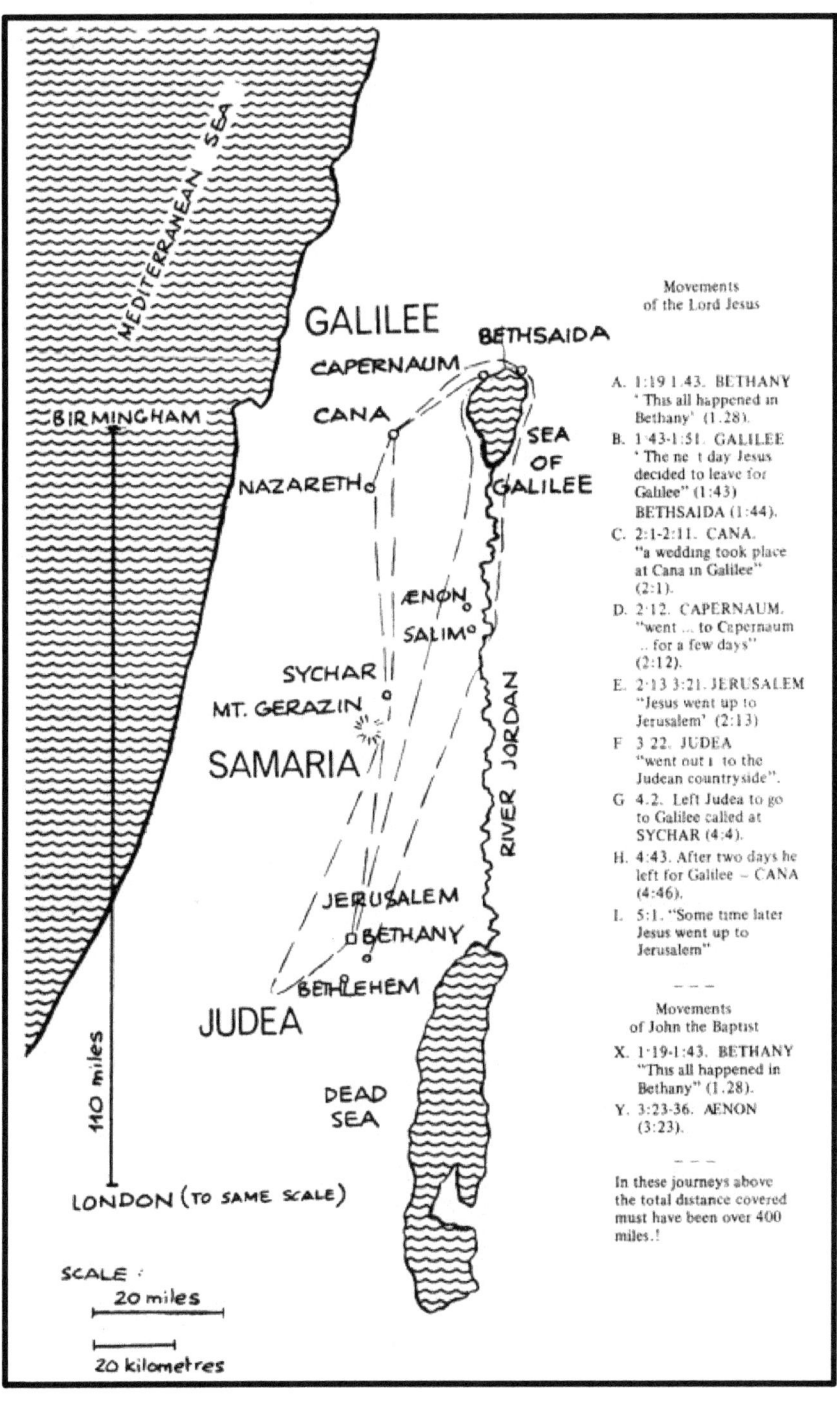

Now the Jews who lived in Samaria were attacked and taken captive by the Assyrians about 611 B.C. Those that lived in other parts of the land were attacked and taken captive by the Babylonians under Nebuchadnezzar about 477 B.C. and the temple in Jerusalem was destroyed.

> Sometime after 455 B.C. these people started to return to the land and commenced rebuilding the temple at Jerusalem. Due to certain differences those who had formerly come from Samaria were not allowed to help with the rebuilding of this temple and so they not only built a rival temple at Mount Gerizim but they also set up a rival priesthood. Thus, although being truly Jews, children of Abraham, and being able to call Jacob their father, an irreparable break was made between these Samaritans and the rest of the Jewish nation. By the time the Lord Jesus came, there was a very bitter feud between them. The Samaritans were particularly hostile to any Jew who came from Galilee or some other place in the north, who was on his way to worship at the temple in Jerusalem – i.e. not going to worship at the Samaritan temple at Mt. Gerizim. Now, it was not necessary to go through Samaria but it was generally quicker and for a Samaritan to help a Jew on the road to Jerusalem was exceptional. This may well add more meaning to the parable of the Good Samaritan, Luke 10:30-35. Also, since the Jews and Samaritans were archenemies and some Jews preferred a Roman to a Samaritan, the woman's question, "You are a Jew and I am a Samaritan woman. How can you ask me for a drink?" is very understandable.

62. What was the gift of God the Lord Jesus referred to?
   A. From verse 10 it is the living water which gives a person everlasting life, verse 14. To obtain this water all one has to do is believe in Him, for we read in John 6:35, "… he who believes in me will never be thirsty".

63. What type of water did the Lord Jesus offer the woman and how does it differ from ordinary water?

A. See the previous answer and note that those who drink ordinary water will need to drink again, but once a person has received the Lord Jesus Christ ... it is a once and for all act which need not be repeated, and, in fact, cannot be repeated.

64. Did the Samaritan woman understand what this water was?

A. From verse 15 it is clear that the Samaritan woman did not understand this beautiful figure of speech. If she had known her Scriptures, she would have known that "Man does not live by bread alone" (Deuteronomy 8:3). True, for some the motto of life is "Let us eat and drink, for tomorrow we die" (Isaiah 22:13) and this may well describe the woman. True a person who believes will still need literal food and drink, but one who knows the Lord Jesus will have found true satisfaction in life. Such a person should never crave after the things of this life. Such a person should be content, and will be so if he is enjoying to the full this spiritual life which is found only in Christ.

65. In what special way must God be worshipped?

A. When reading verses 20-24 please note answer 61 above. There was good reason for the Jews to worship God in His temple, as some of the Old testament contains what should be done there, but on more than one occasion they allowed their worship there to become corrupt (see Isaiah Chapter 1 and note verses 10-24), and this shows how empty the whole system of ritual could become. As for us today, we cannot apply the Jerusalem temple procedure with its animal sacrifices etc. to our way of life and God has never instructed us to do so. Even those for whom it was intended lost the important point "God is spirit, and his worshippers must worship him in spirit and in truth". Places are very secondary to this.

66. Who did the Lord Jesus say He was?

A. From verses 25 and 26 He said He was the Messiah, the Christ.

67. What three descriptions did the Samaritan woman use of the Lord

A. Verse 9 a Jew
Verse 19 a Prophet
Verse 29 the Christ

When she first met the Lord Jesus, she regarded Him as an ordinary Jew but after listening to Him, she said "I can see that you are a prophet". After more words the woman's opinion was that He was the Christ and the people of her area became convinces that He was "The Saviour of the World". – verse 42.

68. What did the Lord Jesus say His food was?
A. Read verse 34.

70. Why did the Samaritans first believe?
A. From verse 39 it is clear that the woman's testimony was the reason they first believed but note verses 41 and 42:

"And because of His words many more became believers. They said to the woman 'We no longer believe just because of what you said; now we have heard for ourselves, and we know that this man really is the Saviour of the world'".

We may be like these, first believing because of what another says but later, knowing for ourselves. They heard His words and believed and today His words are heard through the Scriptures and so we pray that the reader is growing not only in knowledge but also in faith and trust in Him.

69. For what is the crop harvested?
A. Eternal life – verse 36.
Verse 35 states that at that time the fields were ripe for harvest and this cannot refer to the present mission field but to the expectation at that time of a national repentance on the part of Israel. In verses 36-38 the Lord Jesus is pointing out that, although the reaper deserves a reward, he could not have done so without the initial work of the sower. He reminds His disciples that their success owes much to the work of others.

71. After knowing the Lord Jesus, who did the men of Samaria believe Him to be?

    A. Read verse 42 –

"The Saviour of the world".

72. What was the Lord's second miracle in Galilee?

    A. Read verses 46-54.

Note the words of verse 48 which were a warning to some. True belief, true faith "is being sure of what we hope for and certain of what we do not see", Hebrews 11:1; yet, continually, some wanted miraculous signs to support their faith. To these the Lord's words to Thomas are appropriate, "Blessed are those who have not seen yet have believed", John 20:29.

73. What was the result of that miracle?

    A. From verse 53,

"So he and all his household believed".

ANSWERS WITH QUESTIONS: CHAPTER 5

74. What was the man's reply to the Lord's question?

    A. The man's reply to the question "Do you want to get well?" is found in verse 7 and may appear rather strange. However, at that time there was a common superstition that "From time to time an angel of the Lord would come down and stir up the waters. The first one into the pool after such a disturbance would be cured of whatever disease he had". The man evidently held this view and his reply to the Lord Jesus' question will now be appreciated. Perhaps the man thought that the Lord Jesus was going to help him into the pool.

75. What was the Lord's next miraculous sign?

    A. Read verses 5-15 and note verse 9.

Here the man was completely cured at once. This shows how immense the healing power of the Lord Jesus was. The words of verse 14: "Stop sinning or something worse may happen to you" seem to imply that there was a connection between the man's illness and his moral life, although exactly what this was is not clear.

76. Why did the Jews in Jerusalem get annoyed with the Lord Jesus and want to persecute Him?

A. Verse 16.

"Because Jesus was doing these things on the Sabbath, the Jews persecuted him". Please note, however, that the Lord Jesus was NOT breaking the Sabbath Law of the Old Testament but merely breaking a forced and false interpretation of passages, such as Jeremiah 17:21, which had been made by the religious leaders. They made the carrying of anything from a public place into a private house, and vice versa, unlawful. It was not God's law.

77. Why did they want to kill Him?

A. In verse 17 the Lord Jesus said,

"My Father is always at his work to this very day, and I, too, am working".

From verse 18 it is obvious that the Lord Jesus was calling God His own Father and in so doing was making Himself equal with God, i.e. saying He was God.

There are some today who try and make the case that the Lord Jesus Christ is not God. They try and give Him a subordinate role. They say that the Lord Jesus never claimed He was God but all that these people show is their lack of knowledge of the Old Testament Scriptures and their ignorance of what expressions meant in New Testament times. Here, for example, the reaction of the Jews makes it abundantly clear what the Lord Jesus Christ was saying of Himself, "... he was even calling God his own Father, making himself equal with God".

78. Why has all judgment been given to the Son?

A. Again – note in verse 23 the equality of the Father and the Son. Judgment has been entrusted to the Son "that all may honour the Son just as they honour the Father who sent him".

Thus we can see why it is so important to have the personality of the Lord Jesus Christ correct and clear in our beliefs. "The Word was God".

79. How does a person cross from death to life?

A. From verse 21 it is clear that the "life" is something much more than physical life, and "whoever hears my words and believes him who sent me has eternal life and will not be condemned; he has crossed from death to life" – verse 24.

The words "hear" and "believe" in these verses cannot refer merely to intellectual knowledge. True faith and belief in the Lord Jesus will cause a person to put their complete trust in Him and *act* on what is learnt about the Lord Jesus.

80. What do verses 19 to 30 say about resurrection?

A. Verse 21 "…the Father raises the dead and gives them life…"
Verse 25 " the Son of God and those who hear will live".
Verse 28 "…all who are in the graves will hear his voice and come out…"

There are two important points to note here:

(a) Life –i.e. eternal life – is given to believers when they have been raised from the dead. Now they have the promise of the resurrection. Scripture likens death to a sleep and the resurrection is an awakening.

(b) Note that all are raised. Some to eternal life and some will be condemned to the second death – i.e. will not see that life John 3:36 and Revelation 20:11-15.

81. Why is the Lord Jesus Christ's judgment just?

A. Judgment is important and occurs in this chapter in verse 22 where it states that the Father "has entrusted all judgment to the Son" and in verse 30 the Lord Jesus says "I judge only as I hear, and my judgment is just, for I seek not to please myself but him who sent me".

"My judgment is just" is an important point to think about. God is called "The Righteous Judge" and every person will come before Him, as verse 28 makes clear, for assessment. He makes the assessment, He distributes justice and His decisions are 100% correct. Now this is difficult for fallible human beings to appreciate. We know how frail our Courts of Justice are but here we have the One who cannot lie, the One who makes no mistakes; here we have God. Thus, when people ask what is going to happen on the day of reckoning to people in China or darkest Africa, or people who have been brainwashed against Christianity, or people brought up in the religions of the East, or people who are mentally deranged, or people like Judas, or, we may not be able to give an absolute answer but we do know that the Lord Jesus Christ is a God of love and that these people will be dealt with fairly and squarely. One of the things we are told not to do is "judge others". When we try to do this we create problems and difficulties for ourselves – as well as doing it badly. We would do well to remember that all judgment has been entrusted to the Son and that His judgments are just. No one will be treated unfairly.

82. How could the Jews know that the Father has sent the Son into the world?

    A. "I have a testimony weightier than that of John. For the very work that the Father has given me to finish, and which I am doing, testifies that the Father has sent me" verse 36.

Again we must remember that this would have been clear to the Jews who were alive at that time. Read Luke 7:16-23 and note the following:

John the Baptist sent his disciples to ask the Lord Jesus: "Are you the one who was to come, or should we expect someone else", verse 20. The Lord Jesus did not reply but simply asked them to tell John what they had seen. John, who knew his Scriptures, would realise that these miracles were signs which fulfilled the prophecies concerning the Messiah, the Christ. (See, for example, Isaiah 29:18; 35:4-6; 60:1-3). Thus the evidence was not that they were miracles but that they were the miraculous signs which had been prophesied. Thus it is that the Lord Jesus could say "... the very work that the Father has given me to finish, and which I am doing, testifies that the Father has sent me". The Jews, if they had known their Scriptures like John the Baptist, would have known this. However, there was to come an even greater work which was to be an even greater testimony.

83. Can the Bible give a person eternal life?
A. Mere intellectual knowledge of what is written in the Scriptures will not save anyone. Verse 39 shows that Bible study alone cannot give eternal life. Just because a person or a group or a society or an organisation or a book uses the Bible or refers to it ... well, that does not prove anything. Even the Devil can quote the Bible; see Luke 4:10, 11.

84. Can the Bible help a person find how to obtain eternal life?
A. A person or a group or a society, etc., may use the Bible to find out the claims, the teachings and promises of the Lord Jesus Christ. They may use the Bible to get to know Him and to find out what He has done, is doing and will do. Thus, the Scriptures testify of the Lord Jesus Christ and as such can be used to bring a person to Him so that life may be received.

85. Should a believer feel satisfied with human praise?
A. It would appear not. Read verses 41-44.

86. Did all the Jews believe what Moses wrote?
A. Read verses 45-47. No. Some did, but these did not.

If one believes the Lord Jesus Christ, one must believe what Moses wrote, for the Lord Jesus believed Moses to be correct. Moses is referred to in John 3:14 and if any did read the full account in Numbers 21:4-9 they might have found it hard to believe. However, do not forget that this miraculous sign at the time of Moses was to foreshadow the great miraculous sign which is to happen later in the book we are studying. Thus, a serpent on a pole giving longer earthly life to all who looked upon it is but a foreshadowing of Christ the Saviour on a Cross giving eternal life to all who believe in Him. When viewed in this light, the miracle of Moses' time is small.

ANSWERS WITH QUESTIONS: CHAPTER 6

87. Did the Gentiles observe the Passover?
A. It is clear from verse 4 that the Passover was strictly a Jewish feast. Some might think they should observe it but nowhere in the Scriptures does it state that the Gentiles were to observe it. This is so with the other Jewish feasts and observances.

88. Was there enough food for the 5,000?
A. After the next miraculous sign of the Lord Jesus, read 9-13, we see that the bits and pieces left over amounted to twelve basketsful, indicating that there was more than enough.

89. What did this miraculous sign provoke the people to say?
A. "Surely this is THE prophet who is come into the world", verse 14. This miracle convinced them that He was *the* Prophet they had been expecting.

90. What did the people want to do with the Lord Jesus?
A. "They intended to come and make him king by force", verse 15.

91. Did the Jews who followed the Lord Jesus to the other side of the lake have their priorities right?
A. No. From verse 15 "they intended to come and make him king BY FORCE" and the Lord Jesus, from whom they could not hide their innermost thoughts, said "I tell you a truth, you are looking for me, not because you saw miraculous signs but because you

ate loaves and fishes. Do not work for food that spoils, but for food that endures to eternal life, which the Son of Man will give you", verses 26 and 27. Again we see people more concerned with earthly things, just as Nicodemus (3:4) and the Samaritan woman (4:15) had at first been. This is understandable and the Lord Jesus will satisfy the earthly needs but the main reason for His first coming was to give people eternal life and equip them for it.

92. What is the Work of God?
A. "The work of God is this: to believe in the One Whom He has sent", verse 29.

Do you want to participate in the work of God? Then, believe in the Lord Jesus Christ. Abraham believed God and as a result was called "The friend of God" James 2:23.

93. Was it a mark of unbelief for the Jews to ask for a sign?
A. Since the time God started to deal with this Jewish nation, He used signs with them. Gideon and his fleece (Judges 6:36-40) the reader may recall from Sunday School or children's Bible Books. In John 6:31 the miraculous sign of the Manna (Exodus 16:9-15) is mentioned and John 3:14 refers to the miraculous sign of Moses' serpent (Numbers 21:4-9).

We read recently (answer 82) how a question from John the Baptist was answered by the working of miraculous signs. The Book of the Acts is full of the miraculous signs worked during that period. The Jews expected them from God's servants and these servants needed them if the Jews were going to listen to them. However, where are these miraculous signs today? We don't use them. Even those who claim they have some form of power or have the gifts or can heal do not come up to what is described in the Acts of the Apostles. Note for example: Acts 28:8-9

"Paul went to see him and, after prayer, placed his hands on him and healed him. When this happened, *the rest of the sick on the island came and were cured*".

Now, if we read on a little further, Paul eventually gets to Rome and, after debating with the Jewish leaders, we come to Acts 28:26-27. These verses are a prophecy of Isaiah declaring that the Jewish nation would not listen to God. Now, what was God going to do? Acts 28:28 states:

"Therefore I want you to know that God's salvation has been sent to the Gentiles and they will listen".

Thus, at this point in time the Jews ceased to be recognised by God and now the Gentiles, who during the Acts period had been dependent upon the Jews, were to be blessed independently of the Jews. This is an important landmark in God's plan for the world. Notice that after this point in time Paul did not heal people. He did not heal his dear friend Timothy. Read 1 Timothy 5:23.

"Stop drinking only water, and use a little wine because of our stomach and your frequent infirmities"

Neither could Paul heal Epaphroditus, who was one of his closet fellow workers: Read Philippians 2:27.

"Indeed he was ill, and almost died. But God had mercy on him, and not on him only but also on me, to spare me sorrow upon sorrow"

Paul's last letter records: "… and I have left Tromphimus sick in Miletus" 2 Timothy 4:20.

Thus we see an absence of miraculous signs in those parts of Scripture written after the end of the Acts period. When God starts dealing with the Jewish nation again, no doubt He will start to show them miraculous signs, but the Greeks ... they looked for wisdom. It is inappropriate for us today to look for those miraculous signs sued for the benefit of the Jewish nation and which were gifts for the Acts period. This age, in contrast, is based upon the gifts of apostles, prophets, evangelists, pastors and teachers, Ephesians 4:8 and 11.

94. What is the true bread of heaven?
    A. It is the Lord Jesus Christ. Read verses 32, 33.

95. When do these people start their eternal life?
    A. Verse 39 "... But raise them up at the last day".
Verse 40 "...everyone who looks to the Son and believes in him shall have eternal life and I will raise him up at the last day".
Verse 44 "... I will raise him up at the last day".

It may not be clear to the reader what the last day is or when it is. Is it the last day of this age which ceases with the return of the Lord Jesus Christ who comes to set up a Kingdom of peace on this earth which is to last for 1000 years (called the Millennium), or is it the last day of *this* world which ceases at the end of the Millennium when a new heaven and a new earth will be created? Either way it is in the future and no doubt believers will sleep peacefully until called.

96. Who is the only one to have seen the Father?
    A. Read verse 46 and see 5:37.
    Note also 1:18 and 16 and its answer.

97. Which previous verse in John's Gospel is like verse 47?
    A. There are many, so many. See 1:12 and 13; 3:15-18; 3:36; 5:24; 6:40 and 47. Can you find others?

98. What does the Lord Jesus mean when He uses the figure "eat of the bread"?
    A. The last part of verse 51 states:

"If a man eats of this bread, he will live forever. This read is my flesh, which I will give for the life of this world".

Here we have a three-stage line of argument:

(a) I will give this bread
(b) This bread is my flesh
(c) My flesh is My body which I will give up in death

Thus the Lord Jesus is referring to His literal body and not the bread of what is called the Communion or Lord's Supper.

Similarly, verses 53 and 54, drinking of the blood cannot refer to the wine of that ceremony. Some may think that these verses state that it is necessary to participate in the Lord's Supper to have eternal life. This cannot be right, for the Lord Jesus was speaking to these people long before the time He spent with the twelve in the upper room when they first celebrated that meal. Thus, these people would not and could not have understood His words as referring to that ceremony. What would the Jews have understood by the figure "*eat* the flesh of the Son of Man and *drink* His blood"? Well, the Hebrews used this expression with reference to knowledge. Eating and drinking denoted the operation of the mind in receiving and "inwardly digesting" truth or the words of God. No idiom was more common in the days of our Lord Jesus and even today we talk about "digesting" what a person says and "thirsting" for knowledge. This is how His hearers would have understood Him, for they were familiar with this figure but of the "Communion" they knew nothing and the ceremony of the Last Supper is nowhere mentioned in John's Gospel.

Please compare verses 40, 47, 48 with verses 53, 54. We see that believing on the Lord Jesus Christ is exactly the same as eating and drinking Him. Both produce "eternal life" and they must therefore be the same thing. Also one cannot believe in the Lord Jesus until one knows something about Him. The purpose of

John's writing is given in John 20:31, "But these are written that you might believe that Jesus is the Christ, the Son of God, and that, believing, you may have life through his name". Thus John teaches clearly – eternal life through belief – i.e. faith. Thus, if participation in the rite of the Last Supper is an essential to eternal life, it seems strange that John nowhere mentions it.

Read carefully John 6:32-59. If you find it difficult, do not worry. Note the words of many of the disciples of the Lord Jesus in verse 60, "This is a hard teaching. Who can accept it?"

99. What is the difference between this true bread of heaven and the manna of the Old Testament?
   A. Read verse 58.

100. What was really wrong with this people?
   A. Read verse 64. It was unbelief.

101. What was Peter's confession?
   A. Read verses 68 and 69.

ANSWERS WITH QUESTIONS: CHAPTER 7

102. Why did the Lord Jesus stay away from Judea?
   A. From verse 1 it is clear that there were some Jews who were wishing to take His life. No doubt Satan knew that, for God's plan of redemption to be fulfilled, it was necessary for Christ to fulfill all the Old Testament prophecies, including death on the cross. Thus, if Satan could bring about an early death of the Lord Jesus, he could thwart God's plan. This the Lord Jesus knew Satan was trying to do with the help of misguided human beings (verse 1), but the Lord Jesus knew he would not succeed. Hence we have the words in verse 6, "The right time for me has not yet come", and in verse 8, "... for me the right time has not yet come".

103. Did His own brothers believe in Him?

      A. Read verses 3-5.

104. Why were the Jews amazed?

      A. From verse 15 we see they were amazed because they could not understand how this man had such learning without having studied. The reply of the Lord Jesus should be carefully read (verses 16-19), but note verse 17, "If a man chooses to do God's will, he will find out whether my teaching comes from God or whether I speak on my own!"

      One of the first things a person who wishes to do God's will should do is learn what God has said in His written word, the Bible. Those at that time would have consulted some of the prophets and would have learnt what the Messiah was to do and say when He came. It would be good if we, someday, did the same.

105. Did they know where the Christ was to come from?

      A. From verse 27 it would appear not. Some taught the origin of the Messiah was supposed to be a secret and the Rabbis taught that He would come from Bethlehem and then be hidden – but they did not know where. These and other similar lines were based upon tradition and not *completely* upon the Old Testament and it is therefore not surprising that they were wrong.

106. Why did the crowd try to seize the Lord Jesus?

      A. Read verses 28-30.

107. Why were they unable to do so?

      A. "Because his time had not yet come", verse 30. See also the answer to 102.

108. Which verses help to explain what the Lord Jesus said to the Samaritan woman in John chapter 4?

      A. The Lord's words to the Samaritan woman are in John 4:14 and are, "… whoever drinks the water I give him will never thirst.

Indeed the water I give him will become in him a spring of water welling up to everlasting life".

The words of John 7:37-39 may help to explain what the Samaritan woman heard, "'If a man is thirsty, let him come to me and drink. Whoever believes in me, the Scripture has said, streams of living water will flow from within him'. By this he meant the Spirit, whom those who believed in him were later to receive. Up to that time the Spirit had not been given, since Jesus had not yet been glorified".

The Spirit was given to all believers after the Lord Jesus had been raised from the dead and had ascended into heaven. In the Acts of the Apostles we see that the Spirit manifested Himself by miraculous signs which are not only in the Acts but also in the other books written during the Acts period. At the end of the Acts the Jews were set aside for a long period, Acts 28:26-28, and in the Epistles written after the end of the Acts period the Spirit ceased to manifest Himself in this way. (See also the answer to question 93).

At this point it may be a good idea to give the reader a background to the New Testament with one or two brief comments relating to when the books were written. It may surprise the reader to find out that the order of the books of the New Testament, and indeed the Old, is not the order they were written in. The four Gospels – Matthew, Mark, Luke and John – cover a time from 4 B.C. to 30 A.D.

The only historic book of the New Testament is Acts which covers a time from 30 A.D to 60 A.D. and during this period John wrote three letters (1 John, 2 John and 3 John), Peter wrote two letters (1 Peter and 2 Peter), James wrote one and Jude wrote one, but Paul wrote seven: (Galatians, 1 and 2 Thessalonians, Hebrews, 1 and 2 Corinthians, Romans).

After the end of the Acts period Paul wrote another seven letters, (Ephesians, Philippians, Colossians, Philemon, 1 and 2 Timothy and Titus), and these are of greater importance to us today.

The only other book is Revelation which in its final fulfillment relates to the end of this age.

Please note that the above dates are only approximate and that the exact dates when each letter or book was written are open to much debate but the above outline may serve the reader well in future Bible Study.

109. What were the people saying about the Lord Jesus?
A. Verse 40 "Surely this man is *the* Prophet?
Verse 41 "He is the Christ".
Verse 41 "How can the Christ come from Galilee?"
Verse 42 "Does not the Scripture say that the Christ will come from David's family and from Bethlehem, the town where David lived?"

In Matthew 1:1-17 we see the ancestry of the Lord Jesus back to Abraham and we note David in verse 6. Thus, as well as the Lord Jesus being the Son of God His family line was through David. Also, He was born in Bethlehem, Matthew 2:1, and thus the people's comments in John 7:41 were correct. Where these sadly failed was in not knowing the Lord Jesus sufficiently to realise that He did fulfill those conditions. How often do people criticise yet have insufficient knowledge? How often do people criticise the Lord Jesus Christ or the Bible yet do not know either very well.

110. Had any of the Pharisees put their trust in Him?
A. Well, the Pharisees thought none of their number had put their trust in the Lord Jesus but they were wrong. Nicodemus, who made a shaky start, (see the answer to question 44), speaks up. Maybe not to forcibly, but he is growing in conviction.

Note also how misleading the Pharisees were. In verse 52 they state: "Look into it and you will find out that a prophet does not come out of Galilee", yet if we look into it will find that both Jonah and Hosea came from Galilee and probably Elijah, Elisha and Amos did so also.

ANSWERS WITH QUESTIONS: CHAPTER 8

111. Is there a record that the Lord Jesus ever wrote anything?
   A. Many great leaders left writings but the Lord Jesus left none. In verses 6 and 8 of this chapter we have the only references to Him writing.

112. What did the Lord Jesus say to the woman who was taken in sin?
   A. Read verse 11 which shows that the Lord Jesus accepts people just as they are but they, in turn, must be prepared to change their ways.

113. What sort of Judge is the Lord Jesus?
   A. Verses 15 and 16 may appear perplexing but they are not. In verse 15 the Lord Jesus states that they judge by human standards, i.e. by external appearances, and thus make superficial judgments. He does not make that sort of judgment. His judgments, verse 16, are in accordance with the Father and are just. (See the answer to question 81). We judge by human standards and as such have difficulty understanding perfect judgment.

114. How can a person not die in their sins?
   A. Read verse 24.
   A person will not die in their sins if they believe that the Lord Jesus is who He claimed to be. If they do not believe they will die in their sins and John 3:36 states that those who do not believe will not have everlasting life – see question 57 and its answer.

115. What is verse 28 referring to?

Manual on the Gospel of John

A. The Lord Jesus is referring to His death on the cross in verse 28 with the words, "WHEN you have lifted up the Son of Man, THEN you will know who I am".

Here He reveals that after His death they would believe the truth of His claims to be God. An obvious case of this is Thomas who, in John 20:28, makes the claim "My Lord and my God" when the Lord Jesus appeared to him after that death and resurrection.

116. Please read verses 12-29 again very carefully. What happened to people who heard the Lord Jesus speak?
    A. "Even as He spoke, many put their faith in Him", verse 30.

117. What are we told about everyone who sins?
    A. Verse 34
    "everyone who sins is a slave to sin".
    Everyone has a power within themselves that makes it easier to do wrong than to do right.

118. How can someone be set free from slavery?
    A. "So if the Son sets you free, you will be free indeed", verse 36.
    Note also verses 31 and 32. Those who hold to His teaching will know the truth and by knowing the truth they will be set free. Some aspects of the truth the Lord Jesus is talking about are the truth about God, the truth about ourselves, the true purpose of life, the true solutions of life's problems. Verse 12 states that the Lord Jesus Christ is the light of this world and those who follow Him "will never walk in darkness but will have the light of life". They will have direction and purpose in life.

119. Who did the Jews claim was their father?
    A. Verse 39 "Abraham is our father".
    Verse 41 "The only Father we have is God Himself".

120. Why were their claims not true?

A. The answer of verse 41 is wrong because the Lord Jesus says to them, "If God were your Father, you would love me ..." (verse 42), and it is obvious that they did not love Him.

In verse 39 the Jews state "Abraham is our father" and their connection with Abraham became the only important thing to many of them. There was the general belief that the great merits of Abraham became manifested in any descendants of Abraham and here the Lord Jesus corrects this error first by challenging it and then by pointing out, verse 40, that their actions were most unlike those of Abraham. In verse 41 there is another reference to their father and because their descendancy from Abraham had been made to look of little spiritual value, they resorted to claiming God Himself as their father, but this was also untrue. The Lord Jesus points out, in verse 42, "If God were your Father, you would love me ..."

We see the error of relying upon human traditions and upon what other men have done. Here the Jews did not realise that to be the true seed of Abraham involved more than just physical descent; reliance upon past deeds and faith of others was futile.

121. Who did the Lord Jesus say was their father?
   A. Read verse 44
   "... your father, the devil ..."

122. Who is the father of lies?
   A. Read verse 44
   "... the devil ... he is a liar, and the father of lies".

123. Was the Lord Jesus guilty of sin?
   A. The Lord Jesus challenged His listeners to prove Him guilty of sin but they couldn't. Read the answer to question 20 again please. There, a little was written about the animal sacrifice which the Jews had been taught.

Another point about this symbolic teaching foreshadowing Christ's complete sacrifice was that the animal had to be without spot or blemish, i.e. free from all imperfections and faults. It was only the blood of a perfect animal that could make atonement for the sin committed. So it is in the final, complete sacrifice. The One who made it had to be without spot or blemish; He had to be free from all faults; He had to be innocent, and so He was. Only in this way could He who knew no sin be made the sin sacrifice for the world. This teaching, although difficult for us, should have been easily understood by the Jews of the first century who had been taught Moses' Law. The words of Peter, who was with the Lord Jesus for over three years, are significant – "He committed no sin, and no deceit was found in his mouth" 1 Peter 2:22.

124. Did Abraham see the Lord's day?

A. Yes, "Abraham saw it", states verse 56, and he could only have seen it by faith. By faith? This may not seem a very satisfactory answer but seek out the letter to the Hebrews and read all of chapter 11. The opening words are: "Now faith is being sure of what we hope for and certain of what we do not see". Now Abraham certainly had great faith and in verses 9 and 10 we read "By faith he (Abraham) made his home in the Promised Land like a stranger in a foreign country; he lived in tents, as did Isaac and Jacob, who were heirs with him of the same promise. For he (Abraham) was looking forward to the city with foundations, whose architect and builder is God".

Thus, God told Abraham about a future city, the Heavenly Jerusalem, and because of his faith in what he had been told he was prepared to live in tents. What else God told him and how he exercised his faith in the light of that further knowledge we cannot always say but no doubt God told him about the Lord's day and just as Abraham had seen that future heavenly city so he had seen that future day when the Lord was on earth. Abraham knew that the promises God had made to him could only be fulfilled if God Himself visited the earth as a man.

Some people have used the reason of faith to explain verse 51, "I tell you a truth, if a man keeps my word, he will never see death". Now obviously many who kept the Lord's words have seen death and thus we are left wondering what this means. Some say if this verse is true then it means that when a believer dies only part of him dies, his body, but some other part lives on and goes to heaven. However, we have seen many times already that eternal life is promised to the believer but it is not given to him until sometime in the future, the day of resurrection. Thus, an explanation like the one above cannot be correct and those, who have seen the error in the above type explanation, yet appreciate the problem given by verse 51, sometimes use the example of Abraham. They say that just as Abraham saw the Lord's day by faith and so saw past his own death so the believer, by faith, sees past his own death into the future and so never really dies. Well, there may be some truth in this and all believers do look into the future and long for the time of perfection to come but the explanation of verse 51 is much simpler than that.

The Greek expression in verse 51 is a bit awkward and is best translated "… if a man keeps my word, he will not die for ever …", i.e. he will not remain dead, he will not be dead forever. A believer does not suffer eternal death because he will have part in the resurrection into life. This simple explanation agrees with what we have learnt from the rest of John's writings. On this Greek expression the margin note of *The Companion Bible* states: "never see death = by no means see death for ever, i.e. by no means see eternal death, because he will have part in the 'resurrection unto life' as declared by the Lord in John 11:25".

125. Why did the Jews want to stone the Lord Jesus?
A. They wanted to stone Him because of the comment in verse 58, "Before Abraham was, I am!"

"I AM" is the offensive expression. Now why does this cause so much offence? The answer lies, again, in the Old Testament and we do not apologise to the reader for the number of references made to it. We could have made more and probably should have but we trust the reader is beginning to realise that a true understanding of the New Testament can only be obtained when the Old Testament is known and understood.

In Exodus 3:13 Moses said unto God, "Behold, when I come unto the children of Israel, and shall say unto them 'The God of your fathers hath sent me unto you'; and they shall say to me, 'What is His name?' what shall I say unto them?"

In Exodus 3:14 God replies "I AM THAT I AM; Thou shalt say unto the children of Israel, 'I AM hath sent me unto you'". In verse 15 God says "This is my name forever".

This may appear a strange name for God yet a moment's thought will make it clear and show why this name is so apt and can fit only God. It is God only who can say at all points of time, past, present and future, I AM. All other beings He created and we ourselves had a point before which we could not have said "we existed", i.e. before we could say "I am". At this point in time we can say "I am" but there will be a time in the future when we shall fall asleep and then we will not be able to say "I am" until our day of resurrection.

Note that the Lord Jesus uses God's exclusive name of Himself, and rightly so. He is God. It was this that caused the Jews to be so upset. He used this expression inverse 24, where the words "The one I claim to be" have been added by the translators. Thus we see another claim by Him to His Godhead.

ANSWERS WITH QUESTIONS: CHAPTER 9

126. Why was the man born blind?
    A. In verse 2 there is the question, "Rabbi, who sinned, this man or his parents, that he was born blind?" At that time there was much discussion about the connection between suffering and sin. Nowadays it is known that venereal diseases in parents, which

can only be caught by indulging in the sin of fornication, can produce physical ailments not only in the parent but also in a child which may be conceived. Blindness is a typical ailment of the child.

The Lord's reply, in verse 3, does not imply that the man and his parents were sinless or perfect but that the blindness was not the consequence of any sin of theirs. The man was blind "so that the work of God might be displayed in his life". Those who know God consider it a great privilege for His work to be displayed in their life. However, some people view this man's blindness as unnecessary and point out that if he could have been healed at this time, why was he not healed earlier. Some who wish to disbelieve in God point out this sort of thing and claim that disasters and troubles which take place in the world today are evidence against God's existence. They state that if He existed and cared He would do something about them.

There are many answers to this point of view and the reader may well be familiar with many of them but we would just like to make four points:

(a) Much human suffering comes from how people treat each other. Selfishness, thoughtlessness, pride, manifest themselves in so many ways and the results of these failures alone are theft, murders, wars, etc. The Lord Jesus Christ came to be an example to people by living the life of love and it is surely true that if mankind learned to love one another this world would become a paradise. If people ignore God's advice and God's example, then they should not blame Him when things go wrong.

When things go wrong because people have failed to follow God's advice, then they simply cannot use these failures to claim that God doesn't care or doesn't exist.

(b) Then there are natural disasters such as earthquakes, floods and famine. Yet people return to flood areas as soon as the flood subsides. Also scientists are discovering geological rifts and faults which run near the earth's surface. These they know will be the sites of earthquakes and have publicised their findings, yet people still build their houses in these areas. As for famines, should these ever be? Some think there is enough food in this world for all, but we have just not learned to share.

(c) Then, when viewing a personal disaster, there is the fact that we cannot see the whole picture. A child may have been knocked off a bicycle and broken a leg. It is so easy to moan and grumble at God letting this awful thing happen, yet worse could so easily have happened. Again, the child may have learnt a lesson from the accident and given up riding. If it had continued riding a bicycle, maybe sometime later a worse accident, or an early death, could have happened.

(d) Having said all this, how do these affect the blind man of this chapter? Having made the above points we could see how God would allow suffering – not cause it – but permit it to happen. Satan is called the prince or ruler of this world and as such must be allowed to cause certain upsets. However, if God does allow a believer to suffer, we can be sure that the problems and pain of that person will not go unnoticed. Paul suffered much, yet in 2 Corinthians 4:17 we read: "For our light and momentary troubles are achieving us an eternal glory that far outweighs them all".

Thus we cannot view the happenings of this life as if nothing came after it. In this life there is much unfairness and inequality. All men are equal in the sight of God, which is important, but all men are not equal in this life from a human standpoint. Thus, whatever we might think about this blind man, we must remember that God is no man's debtor and He will see in eternal life things are balanced and the 'eternal glory' which He will give will make the sufferings of this life appear as "light and momentary troubles".

On another level, we know ourselves that a certain amount of hardship does us good and we may agree with Paul in Romans

5:3, "...we know that suffering produces perseverance; perseverance, character; and character, hope". We realise that the above answer is very limited and the reader will find that a book like *The Problem of Pain* by C.S. Lewis will prove helpful on this subject.

127. How did the Lord Jesus heal the blind man?

A. Read verses 6 and 7.

The Lord Jesus had just said, "As long as it is day, we must do the work of him who sent me. Night is coming, when no one can work". The contrast between day and night is probably used symbolically of the work of the Lord Jesus – night representing the close of His ministry.

128. The man was asked several questions about how he received his sight. What was his answer on each occasion?

A. Notice the man's answers to the various questions put to him. The question of verse 10 is answered in verse 11. There is a question and an answer in verses 12, 15 and 17. The statement of verse 24 causes the reply in verse 25. Two more questions are asked in verse 26 and the man's reply is in verse 27.

How people come to believe in the Lord Jesus Christ and the eternal life He gives is different for each person. There are some who experience instant, or almost instant, conversion and these tend to know the hour or the day when they made a decision. There are others who, instead of going from black to white in one minute, make the transition by going through all the grey regions. Whichever one of these we liken ourselves to we may still have difficulty explaining how it happened and maybe the reply of this man who was once blind, literally, may be suitable for us who were once blind spiritually; "I don't know. I do know one thing: I was blind, but now I see". Remember the first verse of the song 'Amazing Grace'!

129. Did the Pharisees listen to reason?

A. Read verses 14-34 carefully. Note the Pharisees' comment in verses 28 and 29. They should have recognised the Lord Jesus as the Christ by the miraculous signs He was performing but by this time they were hardening their hearts and not listening to reason. In verses 30-33 the man gives them food for thought, yet their response is to hurl insults and throw him out.

Some may think that the words of John 9:29; "we know that God spoke to Moses, but as for this fellow, we don't even know where he comes from", conflict with those of John 7:27, "But we know where this man comes from". It could be that these were different sets of Jews. These in John 9 may not have known of the Lord's background. On the other hand, they may have been implying that they knew Moses was sent by God but this man … they didn't know if God had sent Him, yet He had displayed the miraculous signs foretold of the Christ by the Old Testament's prophets. They deliberately chose not to see them. (See answer 82).

It is interesting to see the confusion there was amongst the Jews concerning the Lord Jesus Christ. We won't go into details but compare the following with one another:

a) John 7:27, 28 and the answer to question 105.
b) John 7:41, 42 and the answer to question 109.
c) John 7:52 and the answer to question 110.
d) John 9:29 and the answer to question 129.

130. What is worse than physical blindness?
   A. Spiritual blindness is worse than physical blindness (read verses 35-41) and so is deliberate blindness (read answers 82 and 129).

We mentioned in the answer to question 52 that the words of John 3:16 cannot be applied to those who have not heard of the Lord Jesus Christ. Again, John 9:41 is saying that those who really are blind, or ignorant of the facts, cannot be found guilty but the Pharisees were not ignorant of the facts. They should have known better and did know better. They were not really blind, they chose to be blind and thus they were guilty.

Note the words of John 9:39, "For judgment I have come into this world, so that the blind will see and those who see will turnout to be blind", and those of John 3:17, "For God did not send his Son into the world to condemn (judge) the world, but to save the world through him". See also John 12:47. There is no contradiction here. *Salvation*, the theme of John 3:17 and 12:47, is the *object* of His coming. *Judgment* is referring to the *effect* of His coming. *Judgment* was *not* the primary reason for His coming but it was the inevitable effect.

ANSWERS WITH QUESTIONS: CHAPTER 10

131. How do thieves and robbers get into the sheep pen?
    A. A thief or a robber does not enter in by the gate but climbs in by some other way. A thief or a robber is someone who does not use the gate. The gate is the Lord Jesus Christ, verse 7, and He is saying in this passage that the only way to eternal life is through Him, verse 9.

132. Will sheep follow these strangers?
    A. Read verses 3-5.

133. Did the people understand the figure of speech used by the Lord Jesus?
    A. Read verse 6.

134. Do you understand this figure of speech?
    A. Although applications of this passage are easy, the interpretation is difficult. The opening 18 verses of this chapter are not easy to understand. The first five verses do not tell us that the Lord Jesus is either the Good Shepherd or the Gate for the sheep. These verses were a common saying or proverb which was well known. The Jews did not need lessons on the care of

sheep, thus when the Lord Jesus referred to the gate, the thieves and robbers, the watchman, the sheep recognizing the shepherd's voice but not that of a stranger, He was giving no great revelation. He was speaking of that which was common knowledge. His listeners were fully acquainted with the facts He brought before them, but it was the application of this saying that was new.

From verses 7 onwards the Lord Jesus made the applications. In verse 7 the reference to the "gate" is applied to Himself and in verse 11 the reference to the "shepherd" is also applied to Himself. This should cause no confusion. The sheep-pens of that day were stone walls, with no roof and had an opening in one wall but had no physical gate. The shepherd slept in that gateway and guarded his sheep with his life. The Lord Jesus is both Gate and Shepherd.

Now what does verse 8 mean? i.e. "All who ever came before me were thieves and robbers". People like Abraham, Moses, David, Isaiah, John the Baptist, "came before" the Lord Jesus but were those thieves and robbers? No - If we look at the context of this saying we see it is directly connected with the preceding chapter where the Pharisees were addressed, were shown to be blind, and to be blind leaders of the blind. In John 8:42-47 these are called the Children of the Devil.

The comparison and contrast in John 10:1-18 is between the Good Shepherd who gave His life for the sheep and the hireling shepherds who fed themselves and neglected their charge. These, no doubt, were the Scribes and Pharisees who also did not enter by the gate. They rejected the Lord Jesus and so proved themselves to be thieves and robbers also.

135. What will the good shepherd do for his sheep?
    A. Read verse 11.

136. Could *anyone* lay down his life for the sheep?

A. From verses 12 and 13 it is obvious that as the hired hand does not own the sheep and cares nothing for them he is not prepared to give his life for them. But the question asked was "*Could* anyone lay down his life for the sheep?" Is there any point in anyone, but the true owner, laying down his life? No. It is only God the Word, the Lord Jesus Christ, the sinless one, who could have laid down His life to make the great and complete sacrifice for sin which enabled us to obtain forgiveness, and thus eternal life. If anyone else had laid down their life, i.e. any being who was not fully God, then the sacrifice could not have been complete and final and we could not obtain forgiveness for our sins. Psalm 49:7 states "None of them can by any means redeem his brother, nor give to God a ransom for him" and this is so because one sinner cannot redeem another – a sinner cannot even redeem himself. Thus it is that those who teach that the Lord Jesus is not God manifest in the flesh but some lesser being, the ideas vary from His being the Archangel Michael down to a mere man, usually have in their philosophy the need to do something extra to obtain eternal life: e.g. as well as believing one may have to give 10% of one's earnings to the society, or one may have to sell a certain number of books, or attend a certain number of meetings, or do certain specified charitable tasks. We can see that these ideas are not in accordance with what we have read in John's Gospel, 3:16, 36, and so we must disagree with them and firmly state our belief in Christ's Godhead and the eternal life which is freely given to those who have faith in Him. These are the foundations of God's revelation to man.

137. What does the Lord Jesus Christ have to say about His death?
A. Verse 17 "… I lay down my life-only to take it up again".
Verse 18 "… I have authority to lay it down and authority to take it up again".

This ability to take up His life again after death is one of the proofs of Christ's deity because this is an impossibility to mere human beings.

138. Did the Jews accept the Lord's prediction of His resurrection?

A. No. From verses 19-21 it appears, yet again, that their only action is to hurl abuse. See how they did a similar thing in John 8:27-34.

139. Did the Gentiles keep the Feast of Dedication?

A. No. From verses 22-24 we see that only Jews are there. This feast commemorated the cleansing of the temple after its defilement by Antiochus Epiphanes in 164 B.C. In fact the Gentiles were not allowed into the temple. They were only allowed into the outer court, the court of the Gentiles. The barrier of the dividing wall (Ephesians 2:14) separated the two courts and if any Gentile passed that wall the penalty was death. (See diagram below)

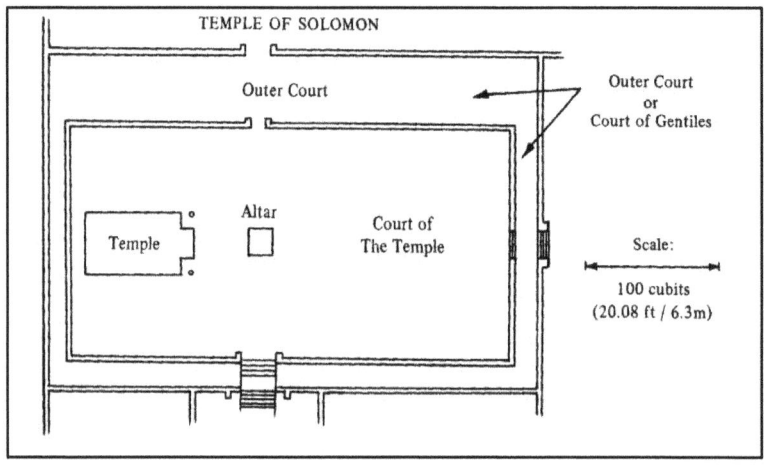

140. Did the Lord Jesus plainly admit that He was the Christ?

A. The Jews asked the Lord Jesus to tell them plainly if He was the Christ, verse 24, and from His reply in the following verse He had obviously done so; compare 4:26 and 9:35-37. He was also performing the miraculous signs which the prophet had said the Messiah would do; see also 5:36, 7:31, 9:32 and 15:24. However, the sad thing was that these Jews did not believe. Their leaders were more concerned with their position in society and keeping in with the Romans, John 11:48. Thus they were following thieves and robbers and did not know the voice of the shepherd. Read verses 1-18 again and note verses 3 and 4 and compare them with verse 27.

141. What does the Lord Jesus, the Good Shepherd, do for His sheep?

A. Verse 28 not only states that He gives them eternal life and that they shall never perish – i.e. not perish forever (see answer 124), but also that, having put them in the position of His sheep "No one can snatch them out of my hand" – i.e. once He has given them eternal life as a free gift, He will not take it from them. No one can cause them to lose that gift and the Lord Jesus can be eluding only to the enemy, Satan, who would, if it were possible, cause people to lose their eternal life. This God has said is impossible and for this we are thankful. What Satan will do, however, is to try and hinder a child of God. He will try to stop him growing in the knowledge of God and so being able to help others come to a saving knowledge of the Lord Jesus Christ. He will try to cause them to become less interested and to do some unchristian acts and to bring shame on the name of the Lord Jesus, and he does have a certain measure of success, but he can never succeed in separating us from the love of God and the eternal life He has promised.

142. What does the Lord Jesus mean by the statement "I and the Father are one"?

A. The words "I and the Father are one" caused strong reaction from the Jews who "picked up stones to stone him".

Verse 33 makes it clear what the Jews understood by these words" ... you, a mere man, claim to be God".

143. Why did the Jews try and seize the Lord Jesus?

A. They claimed that they were not stoning Him for the miracles, yet, if they had only read and believed what their prophets told them about the work of the Messiah, then they would have realised that the Lord Jesus was the Messiah, was the Christ, was God. This was why, when they were about to stone Him, He referred to these miraculous works, verse 32, and why He made the comments of verses 37 and 38.

144. Did John the Baptist do any miraculous signs?
A. No. Read verse 41.
Note that because all that John had said about the Lord Jesus was true, many believed. Let us be sure all we say about Him is true.

ANSWERS WITH QUESTIONS: CHAPTER 11

145. When the Lord Jesus heard that Lazarus was sick, did He go immediately to help him?
A. No. From verse 6, "… he stayed where he was two more days".

146. What word does the Lord Jesus use to describe death?
A. Verse 11 -
"Our friend Lazarus has fallen *asleep* but I am going there to wake him up".

Verses 13 and 14 make it clear that the Lord Jesus is talking about death and we can see that life after death starts when the Lord Jesus wakes up a person. There is no continuous existence of some part of the person. Death is likened to a sleep and eternal life begins at the awakening, the resurrection. Between death and resurrection for some may be thousands of years, for others it may be only a few; yet for both their sleep is so deep that they do not notice the passage of time. It is like the sleep one has during an operation. A few seconds after the injection we go into a deep, deep sleep and when we wake it seems the next instant – but much has happened and time has marched on.

147. How long was Lazarus in the grave?
A. Verse 17 – four days.

148. What did Martha say to the Lord Jesus?
A. Read verses 21 and 22.

149. Did Martha believe she would see her brother again?

A. The Lord Jesus told her, "Your brother will rise again".

Note that this did not take her by surprise. She answers "I know he will rise again in the resurrection of the last day". She expected to see him at that time, on the day of resurrection. She did not expect to see him when she died but when they would both be raised at the last day.

150. What happens to believers who are dead?

A. Read verses 24-26.

Do you believe this? If the expression "… whoever lives and believes in me will *never* die" causes the reader concern, please see the answer to question 124.

151. "Jesus wept" is the shortest verse in the Bible. Why did He weep"?

A. Some point to the Jews' comment in verse 36, "See how he loved him" and say that the Lord Jesus wept because a very close friend had died. A close reading of this chapter shows that while this is true there is something deeper. Please note the following:

(a) When He heard Lazarus was ill, He says in verse 4, "This sickness will not end in death. No, it is for God's glory so that God's Son may be glorified through it". Thus, some miraculous sign was soon to happen.

(b) "Yet when he heard that Lazarus was sick, he stayed where he was two more days", verse 6. He knew this would lead to deterioration in Lazarus' condition.

(c) He says in verse 11, "Our friend Lazarus has fallen asleep; but I am going to wake him up".

(d) "Jesus had been speaking of his (Lazarus') death", verse 13.

(e) The Lord Jesus says in verse 23, "Your brother will rise again".

(f) He says in verse 25, "I am the resurrection and the life. He who believes in me will live, even though he dies".

In John 10:17, 18 the Lord Jesus says, "... I lay down my life – only to take it up again. No one takes it from me, but I lay it down of my own accord. I have authority to lay it down and authority to take it up again". If He could do this with His own life, He must be able to do it for others also.

In John 11:15 the Lord Jesus says "Lazarus is dead, yet for your sake so that you may believe, I am glad I was not there". Thus He was going to do something that would strengthen their belief in Him, strengthen their faith. So we read in verses 41 and 42, "Father, I thank you that you heard me. I know you will always hear me, but I said this for the benefit of the people standing here, that they may believe that you sent me".

But we have still not answered the question – why did He weep?

The Lord Jesus loved Martha, her sister Mary, and brother Lazarus, yet He purposely refrained from hurrying to help them and when He got there He wept!! This is perplexing. Most certainly there was no lack of heartfelt sympathy with that mourning household and in the heart of the Lord Jesus there was intense love and deep sympathy ... but there was also another feeling.

Verses 33 and 38 record that the Lord Jesus was "deeply moved" and the word so translated means, literally, to snort as a horse does from fear or anger. No doubt, it was anger that caused this deep emotion; anger at sin and the death it causes and the sorrow death brings. He may have wept when He saw the sorrow sin and its result, death, caused amongst those whom He loved.

The figure of a snorting horse indicates the animal's impatience to get going and this, used of God, would be just as understandable to a Jew as the words "roaring like a lion". Thus, these verses are teaching that the Lord Jesus was moved with deep sympathy. He shared the grief of those who mourned their loved one but He was grieved more by sin and its consequences upon those He loved than by the actual death, because as He turned to the grave which contained the evidence of the work of Satan, the Lord Jesus not only wept but, like a war horse, he scented the battle with the Enemy who had the power of death, Satan. Here the Lord Jesus anticipated the day of His complete victory; the day of resurrection when not only Lazarus but *all* that are in the grave shall rise.

If any are concerned that the Lord Jesus let Lazarus die and think it unjust, please read the answer to question 126.

152. What did the Lord Jesus say to Lazarus and what happened?
A. Read verses 43 and 44.

153. What was the result of this miraculous sign?
A. Read verse 45,
"Many ... put their faith in him".

154. What were the Pharisees concerned about?
A. Read verse 48.
They were concerned for the nation but they were also selfishly concerned for their own place within that nation. Here was the One who could have freed that nation from Roman bondage but who would not tolerate the behaviour of the Pharisees. Thus if they had been more concerned for the nation, instead of their own position, they would have welcomed Him.

155. What did Caiaphas say would happen to the Lord Jesus?
A. Read verses 50-52.
Note Caiaphas said, "... it is better for you that one man die for the people than that the whole nation perish". No doubt Caiaphas thought that if the people followed the Lord Jesus this would upset the Romans, who might come in force and carry many of the Jews captive to distant parts of the Roman Empire. This had

happened centuries before at the hands of the Assyrians and Babylonians and, although many of the Jews had by this time returned to the land, many were still scattered abroad. These exiled Jews were known as the Dispersion and it is these to whom John refers in the phrase "scattered children of God", verse 52. It is these Jews Paul visited on his journeys during the Acts period. It is these Jews to whom some of the letters of the New Testament are addressed, e.g. James 1:1 "To the twelve tribes scattered amongst the nations".

What Caiaphas' line of thought was, was that if the Lord Jesus was executed, it would be easier for the scattered Jews to return to the land. What he feared was that, if the support for the Lord Jesus increased, the Romans would storm in and scatter the Jews, who were in the land, throughout the Roman Empire. Even though the support for the Lord Jesus amongst the Jews did not grow, that nation was eventually scattered by the Romans.

We have read before that at the end of the Acts period – i.e. after another 30 years of ministry by Peter and the twelve within the land and by Paul and company to the Jews outside the land, the Jewish nation were set aside by God because they continued to refuse the Lord Jesus as their Messiah. The words of Acts 28:26-28 came into force and God allowed the Romans to scatter them. In these days we see this nation gathering again in the land God gave them.

The remarkable thing about Caiaphas' words is that there was a certain amount of truth in them. "It is better for you that one man die for the people than that the whole nation perish". If the Lord Jesus had not come and died (and rose from the dead) then, not only would that nation have perished for eternity, but so would all people. It is the death of that One which enables all believers to have eternal life. Caiaphas did not realise the secondary meaning of what he was saying.

ANSWERS WITH QUESTIONS: CHAPTER 12

156. What did Mary do for the Lord Jesus?
    A. Read verse 3.

157. Was Judas Iscariot's objection well motivated?
    A. No - Read verses 4-6.
    Verse 7 may be perplexing. "'Leave her alone'. Jesus replied, 'It was meant that she should save this perfume for the day of my burial'". Some think these words imply that Mary had some perfume still unused and the Lord Jesus was suggesting that the remainder should be kept to anoint His body at His burial. However, some information may be obtained from Mark 14:1-8 which may not be a record of the same anointing but the circumstances and attitudes of the people are similar. It is Mark 14:8 which is of help, "... she poured perfume on my body beforehand to prepare me for my burial". Thus in John 12 Mary's act was also in anticipation of His burial, which took place just five days later. (Verse 1 states that "*Six* days before the Passover Jesus arrived in Bethany" but as the Jewish day went from sunset to sunset, i.e. from about 6 p.m. to 6 p.m. and not from midnight to midnight, by the time the evening dinner was given in His honour the next day had arrived).

158. Why did the Jews want to kill Lazarus?
    A. Read Verses 10, 11, 17-19.

159. What Old Testament Scripture did the Lord Jesus fulfill on His entry into Jerusalem?
    A. Verse 15 is a quotation from Zechariah, the second to the last, book of the Old Testament. See Zechariah 9:9.

160. Did the disciples realise, at that time, that such prophecies were being fulfilled?
    A. No. Read verse 16, but they did later.

161. Who else were among the Jews who went up to the feast?

A. There were some Greeks, verse 20, who are Gentiles. Anyone who is not a Jew is a Gentile. To find Gentiles among those who went up to worship at the feast may be a surprise to the reader or may cause concern.

From the answer to question 139 we see that the Gentiles were not allowed into the Temple. Thus, who are these "Greeks"? Some may think that this expression refers to Greek speaking Jews, but this is doubtful. It must refer to non-Jews – i.e. Gentiles. Gentiles would be allowed into the Outer Court of the Temple called the Court of the Gentiles and many did go there. They were enquirers about God's revelation of Himself through the Prophets and teachers of the Jews. They would not, however, be allowed to eat the feast of the Passover unless they were Proselytes. If any of these enquiring Gentiles did decide to adopt the Jewish way of life and its worship of God, then they could do so. These were then called Proselytes and were counted as Jews. They could enter the Temple and participate in all the activities of the Jews. Thus the Greeks mentioned here went up to worship at the feast and were most probably Proselytes.

162. What figure does the Lord Jesus use to describe His death and resurrection?

    A. Read verse 24 which again points out the necessity of His death to procure many lives.

163. What did the Lord Jesus say about those who love and hate life?

    A. "The man who loves his life will lose it", verse 25. "While the man who hates his life in this world will keep it for eternal life", verse 25.

This verse is not a message to the unbeliever but it is one to the believer. It was addressed to His followers, namely Andrew and Philip, and similar words were spoken to the disciples in Matthew 16:24-28. These words in Matthew are *not* a gospel message but are an exhortation to those who are already followers. It is an exhortation to them to really give up the life of this world, with its selfish desires, and become fully committed to the Lord Jesus.

We have seen clearly that eternal life is a free gift of God to whoever believes in the Lord Jesus. Thus the words of Matthew 16:27 "... then he will *reward* each person *according to what he has done"* must refer to the service and sacrifice of the follower of the Lord Jesus. There can be *no* reward to those who don't believe for they do not have eternal life, John 3:36, but the believer ... as well as eternal life, he may also be given a reward according to what he has done; he will be given a reward provided he hates the selfish aspects of life in this world and becomes fully committed to the life which is in Christ Jesus our Lord.

164. Did the Lord Jesus want to be saved from His hour of death?

A. Most definitely not! Read carefully His words in verse 27, "Now my heart is troubled, and what shall I say? 'Father save me from this hour? No, it was for this very reason I came to this hour. Father glorify your name".

Thus the Lord Jesus here points out that His heart is troubled and what can He say ... 'Will I say, "Father save me from this hour"? Most definitely not. I will say, "Father, glorify your name ..."'".

This is what the Lord Jesus is saying.

165. Did the Lord Jesus know what kind of death He was to suffer?

A. Yes. Read verses 32 and 33.

In verse 31 the Lord Jesus had just stated, "Now the prince of this world will be driven out". The term "prince of this world" obviously cannot refer to the Lord Jesus. It was a well-known Rabbinical term for Satan and in verse 31 the Lord spoke of the defeat of Satan and his works of sin and death. The victory over Satan, sin and death was achieved by the Lord Jesus in His death and resurrection but it has not yet been fully inflicted and will not be until the Lord Jesus returns.

The words "Now is the time for judgment on this world" could also be linked with the Lord's death and resurrection and the judgment He is to inflict on the world by them. However, these words could mean that a crisis had been reached at that time because the world was about to pronounce judgment against the Lord Jesus and His claims.

"But I, when I am lifted up from the earth, will draw all men to myself" are the words of verse 32. They do not mean that the Lord Jesus will forcibly draw all men to believing in Him. However, that death on the cross does enable all men to be drawn away from the bondage of Satan and towards the Lord Jesus. The result of this drawing is not stated and for some it is the gift of eternal life but for others, in view of the words of verse 21, it will result in judgment and condemnation, John 3:17-18.

166. Did the crowd think that the Christ would remain forever?
A. Yes, verse 34, but we must remember that the only Scriptures the Jews had were those we call the Old Testament. Also they had two disadvantages compared to us:

(a) We all have God's written word to read.

(b) We can look back upon Christ's completed work on the cross.

Now the Old Testament makes it clear that the Messiah, the Christ, had two roles. One indicating suffering, and the other indicating glory and reigning. The Jewish leaders could not understand how these two roles could be combined and, preferring the latter one, looked only for the victorious Messiah ruling an everlasting kingdom. This may account for their rejection of the Lord Jesus Christ, and for the question asking of the Christ was to remain forever.

It may also explain the people's action in John 6:15 when they tried to "make him king by force" and also the words of John 7:27. When the victorious, glorious and reigning Christ comes, no one will know where He comes from.

We look back and see that these two roles of the Messiah will be fulfilled by two visits of the Lord Jesus Christ – one was in the past when He suffered and went away; the other when He will come and rule over the earth and remain is still future.

167. How does one become a son of light?
A. By putting one's trust in the light, verse 36. Read John 1:6-9; 8:12; 9:5.

168. What prophet of the Old Testament predicted the attitude of the Jewish leaders to the Lord Jesus?
A. It was the prophet Isaiah (53:1) who had previously used the words of verse 38 but it is the words of verse 40, quoted from Isaiah 6:9 and 10 which are important.

These words of Isaiah were first quoted by the Lord Jesus in reply to the disciples' question "Why do you speak to them in parables?" Matthew 13:10-14. Here the Lord Jesus warned the people with the words of Isaiah about their attitude towards Him and His teaching.

These words of Isaiah are next used here in John 12:40 where another warning is given because the Jews continued in unbelief.

These words of Isaiah are used just once more: in Acts 28:26 and 27. This time they are not used as a warning but are given as the reason why the Jewish nation had been set aside by God. They are followed by the words, "Therefore I want you to know that God's salvation has been sent to the Gentiles, and they will listen".

The Old Testament reveals that the Jews acting as a Kingdom of Priests would bring the Gentiles into a knowledge of God. This was what was happening in the last half of the Book of Acts, but the Jewish nation were proving so difficult to use, because of their unbelief and continued rejection of the Lord Jesus by most of them that God laid them aside and Acts 28:28 teaches that God's salvation is now to be sent to the Gentiles independently of the Jews. This is why some of the teaching after the end of the Acts period is different, but please note that not all teaching changes – e.g. the great truth of eternal life through faith in the Lord Jesus Christ does not alter.

169. Why had the prophet predicted these things?
A. Read verse 41 and compare it with John 8:56. Read also the answer to question 124.

170. What difficulties did those leaders who wanted to confess their faith in the Lord Jesus have put in front of them?
A. Read verse 42 but note especially verse 43.
How we could apply these verses to us today! Many leaders attended the religious establishment of their day, then discovered the *true* way of life, yet they still wanted to attend synagogues which had their priorities wrong and taught much that was not true. These people also loved the praise of men.

We cannot criticize them. We all like praise from others and we know that it is difficult to break old habits.

171. Is it possible to have real belief in the Lord Jesus without a belief in the Father?
A. No. Read verse 44. Yet there are some who claim a person can be a Christian and not believe in God!

172. Does it matter that no one has seen God in His essence as Spirit?
A. No. Read verses 44 and 45. The Lord Jesus came for many reasons. One thing mankind has always wanted to do is see God and know what He looks like. Thus, many pagans set up images

Manual on the Gospel of John

– But God would never allow Israel to do this. So, we may ask, how can we think of God? How do we imagine Him? An old man with a beard? No – when we look on the Lord Jesus Christ we look on the One who sent Him. Thus, those who see the Lord Jesus Christ as God have no problem but those who see Him as a separate being still wonder needlessly, what God is like.

173. What was the purpose of the Lord Jesus Christ's first coming?
   A. Read verse 46.

174. Did He come to judge the world?
   A. No. Read verse 47 – and the answer to question 130.

175. What happens to those who reject the Lord Jesus?
   A. Read verse 48.

Please note the answer to question 52. This answer was commenting upon John 3:15-18 which we said could only refer to those who have heard of the Lord Jesus Christ. The words of John 12:48 point this out clearly for one can only reject what one has seen or heard.

ANSWERS WITH QUESTIONS: CHAPTER 13

176. When did the events of this chapter take place?
   A. From verse 1, it was just before the Passover Feast. For details of the institution of the Passover, read Exodus 12. Briefly, there was to be a death in every home in the land of Egypt. It was to be either the first-born – i.e. the eldest child, or it was to be a lamb – i.e. a substitute. The Jews killed the lamb and put its blood on the doorposts and above the door. In any home which did not do this, the first-born died.

One of the titles of the Lord Jesus in the Scriptures is "our Passover" and speaks of Him being sacrificed. He is viewed as the lamb whose blood saved that member of the household. "We have now been justified by his blood" – Romans 5:9.

177. Who promoted Judas Iscariot to betray the Lord Jesus?
   A. Read verse 2.

178. Was the Lord Jesus above doing the work of a slave or servant?
   A. No. Read verses 4 and 5 and note also verses 14-17. Neither should we be above doing menial tasks for others.

179. Was Peter impetuous?
   A. Just from reading verses 6-9 and noting in verses 21-25 how Peter spoke up when the others did not, it would appear to indicate that he was impetuous.

Peter is an interesting character and throughout the New Testament we see his character depicted and not only are the good points brought out. Read Matthew 16 where in verses 13-20 we see Peter at his best, but when the Lord Jesus mentioned His future death and resurrection, Peter's remark brought him a sharp rebuke – verses 21-23.

Again we remember how it was Peter who wanted to walk on the water but in the end cried out for help – Matthew 14:22-36. It was Peter who spoke up and said he would lay down his life for the Lord Jesus but was told that he would deny Him three times – John 13:36-38.

In John 21:3-11 the Lord Jesus appeared to the disciples after His resurrection. When they realised it was Him, it was Peter who jumped into the water to get to Him quickly. The others followed.

In Galatians 2:11-21 we see that Peter had to be corrected by Paul. And there are other examples of weaknesses in this man's character; yet he was given the task of preaching the gospel to the Jews – Galatians 2:7. Note here that Paul had been given the task of preaching the gospel to the Gentiles.

We mention these things about Peter to show how great God is to use such human beings. We all have our weaknesses but these should not stop us witnessing for Him. We suggest that much can be learnt by studying the characters of the Bible – i.e. Abraham, Moses, David, and Paul.

180. What should the Lord Jesus be called by those who follow Him?
A. Read verses 13 and 14.
He should be called Lord and teacher.

Throughout this work we have mostly referred to Him as LORD Jesus. We feel this is the correct way to address Him. Jesus on its own fails to indicate that, not only have we come to know Him as Saviour, but He is also our Lord and Master and we are striving to go on with Him.

He is also a teacher. When on earth, we see He was limited in the sense that He was to fulfill all that the Old Testament had said about Him. His work can be better appreciated and understood by those who know the teaching given by God to the Jews and recorded in the Old Testament. One limitation, for example, is seen when He says "I was sent only to the lost sheep of the house of Israel" – Matthew 15:24. Similarly He told His disciples during the gospel period, "Do not go among the Gentiles or enter any town of the Samaritans. Go rather to the lost sheep of Israel" – Matthew 10:5.

His death was for the world. The way He lived His life was an example to the world. But, when on this earth, He was a teacher of Israel. However, we must not assume that the only teaching the Lord Jesus gave is contained in the Gospels. These record His words whilst here on earth. Paul states that his teaching was from the Lord Jesus Christ who had ascended to the right hand of God. Thus we see that we have the teaching of the Lord Jesus revealed to the Gentiles through the Apostle Paul, Galatians 2:7. Some is different from what He taught the Jews; much is the same.

It may be that the reader still thinks that the words of the Lord Jesus in the Gospels are more important than the words of the apostles in their letters or epistles. This would be true if they *were* the words of the apostles, but they are not. They are the words of the ascended, glorified Christ.

181. Is a servant greater than his master?
A. No. Read verse 16.
In this chapter we see the disciples being prepared for the great work they were to do during the Acts period. In those years we read that they were to perform greater miracles than the ones performed by the Lord Jesus – John 14:12. Thus, as frail human beings, it would be possible for them to become filled with self-importance and have an exaggerated opinion of their position. So it is that this verse is a call for humility and follows the section on foot washing – verses 1-14, which is an act of lowliness. If He, their Lord, teacher, master and the one who sent them, would do this for them, then they, the servants, messengers, must be prepared to do it for one another – verses 14-16. Humility is necessary for blessing – verse 17.
one who sent me."

182. Which Old Testament Scripture is next fulfilled?
A. Read verse 18. It is a quotation from Psalm 41:9.

183. What is the purpose of predicting events?
A. Read verse 19 and note John 14:29. Verse 20 indicates that, when a person accepts the Lord Jesus Christ, he also accepts the One who sent Him.

184. Did the disciples, at that time, realise what Judas was about to do?
A. No. Read verses 28 and 29.
Note than in verse 23, "The disciple whom Jesus loved" refers to John, the writer of this Gospel – see John 21:20-24. It was John who asked the question in verse 25.

185. When did Satan enter Judas?
A. "As soon as Judas took the bread, Satan entered him" – verse 27.

What exactly happened here is difficult to understand but let us look at the whole context.

(a) The words of the Lord Jesus in verse 21 "I tell you a truth – one of you is going to betray me" caused the disciples to be somewhat perplexed – verse 22.

(b) "The disciple whom Jesus loved" was nearest the Lord Jesus – verse 23 – and Peter, who was some way away, motioned for John to ask the Lord Jesus "which one he means".

(c) John asked the Lord Jesus – verse 27 – and was told "it is the one to whom I will give the piece of bread when I have dipped it in the dish". The other disciples may not have heard this. However:

(d) At that point in time, Judas was free to repent. Satan had put the thought of betraying the Lord Jesus into his heart, verse 2, but the act was not, at this point, inevitable. However:

(e) Judas took the piece of bread and he knew the symbolism of this act. He had eaten bread with the Lord Jesus and was a close friend but then come the words of verse 27:

(f) "As soon as Judas took the bread, Satan entered him". Judas had passed over the line which divides followers of the light from followers of darkness, but even though Judas was to betray the Lord Jesus, the Lord Jesus did not betray him. Judas had been one of the twelve; he had been one of the two, when the Lord Jesus sent out His disciples in pairs – (Luke 10:1). Nothing indicated that Judas was an adversary, a devil (John 6:70, and as far as we can see from the four Gospels, he spoke with the same authority as the rest of the twelve and worked the same miracles. Thus he had every opportunity and encouragement to repent.

(g) Even after the words of verses 26, 27 the disciples did not even suspect Judas. He must have been highly regarded and was in charge of the money and so was trusted. Thus the others supposed he had gone out "to buy what was needed for the feast or to give something to the poor", verse 29.

186. When did Judas leave the Lord Jesus and the eleven?
A. At night – verse 30 – after he had taken the bread – verse 27.

187. Who is to be glorified?
A. (a) "Now the Son of Man is glorified and God is glorified in him.

(b) If God is glorified in him then God will glorify the Son in himself and will glorify him at once".
Verses 31 and 32.

After Judas had gone the Lord Jesus knew that His time had come, verses 1-3 and 31, 32. From one point of view that time was the saddest and blackest in the whole of human history, for it saw the rejection, betrayal and crucifixion of the Son of God; the one who is our "Great God and Saviour, Jesus Christ" (Titus 2:13).

However, here we do not find the spirit of doom, despondency or disgust but we see five references to "glory". Now what exactly "glory" is may be hard to define and a reading of John 17:1-5 may throw a little more light on the subject, Thus John 13:31, 32 does not give us cause for gloom or despair. Here the Lord's statement is in two sections:

(a) The first is governed by the present "now"
"NOW is the Son of Man glorified and God is glorified in him" – verse 31.
(b) In the second is governed by the future "will"
"if God is glorified in him,
then God WILL glorify the Son in himself
and Will glorify him at once" verse 32.

These refer to His approaching death and the finishing of the work He had come to do which involved His glorious resurrection from the dead which was the victory over death and its sting, sin (1 Corinthians 15:54-57).

John 17:1-5 is of help for it shows that:

(a) In the first section of John 13:31 and 32 we have the fact that in His death the Lord Jesus was glorified and that, in that death, the Father was glorified.

(b) In the second section of John 13:31 and 32 we have the fact that in the resurrection and the present place of the Lord Jesus at the Father's right hand both the Son and the Father are glorified.

188. What new commandment was given to the disciples?
   A. Read verse 34.
   Note that it says "Love one another. *As I have loved you,* you must love one another". Read 1 Corinthians 13 to see what this love involves.

189. How were people to know His disciples?
   A. Read verse 35.

ANSWERS WITH QUESTIONS: CHAPTER 14

190. Will the Lord Jesus come back for the disciples?
   A. Yes. Verse 3.
   Some may think that this refers to the Lord's return from death and resurrection but this is not so. In John 11:24 we read that Martha knew her brother Lazarus would rise again on the last day. The day of resurrection for the disciples is when the Lord Jesus returns.

191. What was the way to the place the Lord Jesus is talking about?
   A. Thomas did not know so he asked the way and the answer the Lord Jesus gives is "I am the way – and the truth and the life. No

one comes to the Father except through me", verse 6. This is not unlike John 10:1-21. Please read those verses again.

192. How does one get to see the Father?
A. Read verses 7-15 and note particularly verse 7, "If you really knew me, you would know the Father as well", and verse 9, "Anyone who has seen me as seen the Father". Note verses 10 and 11 and see also answers 96 and 173.

193. Would the disciples do greater things than the Lord Jesus?
A. The simple answer is yes, and comes from reading verse 12, which refers not only to miracles (see for example Acts 5:15; 19:11 and 12; 20:9, 10), but also to a greater, more extended and successful ministry. The Lord Jesus rarely went outside the land of Palestine and He forbade the twelve, during the Gospel period, to go to any other than the lost sheep of the House of Israel, Matthew 10:5 and 6. However, during the Acts period, they went much further afield, Acts 8:4, and Paul stated that "your faith is being reported all over the world", Romans 1:8. Nonetheless, some further comments need to be made.

In verse 11 we read, "Believe in me when I say that I am in the Father and the Father in me; or *at least* believe on the evidence of the miracles themselves". We saw a similar appeal to these miraculous signs in John 10:38. The reason for this was that the Old Testament prophets had clearly indicated what the Messiah, the Christ would do. Thus the Lord Jesus Christ had restricted Himself by what had been said centuries earlier to the prophets.

However, after He had been raised from the dead and had ascended, another Counsellor, the Spirit of truth, was given to the disciples and also the ability to perform many miraculous signs. Please read the Acts of the Apostles. They healed all sicknesses; they raised people from the dead, etc. and it was necessary for them to be able to perform these signs which were needed to convince the Jews that God had sent these disciples and followers. Thus, throughout the Acts period, i.e. the record of events contained in the Book of Acts itself and the letters or epistles written during that time, there are many references to miraculous signs – but in the letters written after the end of the Acts period we see this ability to perform miraculous signs was lost. No, not lost – but withdrawn by God, because miracles were used by Him as a sign to the Jewish nation. That power was no longer needed as the Jewish nation had been set aside at the end of the Acts period, and still is, but one day He will start to work with that nation again.

Some who have not seen this aspect of God's plan have tried in vain to perform some of these miracles. They have not realised that these signs are not needed today. Some who could not produce miracles have thought that they did not have the true faith and unfortunately some have become sad and discouraged.

Others have claimed that they can produce the miraculous signs and say that the above explanation is wrong. However, a close examination of the experience of such people and the results of their efforts will show that their attempts are unlike the true miracles of the Bible. This subject could take much time but just let us consider healing. Some who claim they have this gift today fail to heal the majority of people who come to them and it is doubtful if they ever heal any *completely*; yet Paul, during the Acts period, had complete success. Read Acts 28:8 and 9. "His (Publius) father was sick in bed, suffering from fever and dysentery. Paul went in to see him and, after prayer, placed his hands on him and healed him. When this happened, *the rest of the sick on the island came and were cured*".

No failure here, yet note these three extracts from Paul's letters written after the end of the Acts period:

Philippians 2:26 and 27: "For he (Epaphroditus) longs for all of you and is distressed because you heard he was ill. Indeed he was ill, and almost died. But God had mercy on him, and not on him only, but also on me, to spare me sorrow upon sorrow". Here there is no reference to Paul healing this man. If he could have, then there would have been no need for sorrow. No doubt Paul did not sit around helpless watching his friend slowly die. Naturally he prayed for Epaphroditus but he did not lay his hands on him or perform any miraculous signs. In this new dispensation Paul had to rely wholly upon God's mercy and in this case his friend recovered.

However, in spite of Paul's prayers for Timothy, this friend did not get well.

1 Timothy 5:23: "Stop drinking only water and use a little wine for your stomach and frequent illnesses". No miracles – just advice.

And Paul "left Trophimus sick in Miletus", 2 Timothy 4:20.

Yes. Paul had lost his power to perform miraculous signs but he had not lost his faith. He had understood the change in God's plan and it is his writings which help us Gentiles in so many different ways. He was the apostle to the Gentiles and his last seven letters written after the end of the Acts period are very relevant to today; but, mind you, all Scripture is profitable. (see the answer to question 114).

194. What does verse 14 mean?

A. "You may ask anything in my name, and I will do it" – verse 14. Such passages as this have caused concern to many who have had 'unanswered' prayers but perhaps other passages of Scripture can be of help.

Matthew 21:22, "*If you believe*, you will receive whatever you ask for in prayer" seems to add another angle.

Mark 11:24, "… whatever you ask for in prayer, *believe that you will receive it*, and it will be yours," adds a further one.

In Luke 22:42 our Lord Jesus prays; "… yet not my will but *yours be done"*.

And 1 John 5:14, 15 states, "We have this assurance in approaching God that *if we ask anything according to his will, he hears us*. And if we ask anything that he hears – whatever we ask – we know that we have what we asked for".

Thus, so far we have two necessities – prayers must be from believing hearts and must be in harmony with God's will. Obviously He will give only that which is good and if we faithfully ask but do not receive it means that what we asked for was not His will, was not for the best. Thus, the main problem is ascertaining the Will of God and some fail to realise that His will changed, or it would be better to say, manifested itself in a different way, once the Jewish nation had failed and had been set aside. People's prayers set in the context of the Old Testament period, or the Gospel period, or the Acts period, may contain elements which are of value today but they may not be completely in harmony with God's will for the present period, which began after the end of the Acts period.

Another explanation is similar to the answer to the previous question and links the full explanation of the problem people experience with this verse too much of what was stated there. If the aspect of working greater miraculous signs ceased at the end of the Acts period so, in the same way, could it not be that the promise of giving *anything* asked in His name also ceased?

A further explanation points out that these words were addressed to the disciples and ask if this promise, given to the disciples, can be applied to all believers for all time?

"In my name" is a phrase which also causes concern. The word for "in" can also be translated "through" so that the verse would be "You may ask anything through my name, and I will do it". This may sound a little strange but indicates the Lord's work as mediator. All our prayers should be addressed to the Father but asked through the Son, who is the one mediator between God and man.

195. Who was to be within the disciples?
   A. "The spirit of truth, to be with you forever. The world cannot accept this Counsellor, because it neither sees him nor knows him. But you know him, for he lives with you and will be in you", verse 17.

"On that day you will realise that I am in my Father, and you are in me and I am in you", verse 21.

If the reader moves in different Christian circles, he may well hear statements such as "a believer has Christ dwelling in his heart" or "a believer has the Holy Spirit within him" or "a believer has a new nature". All these are true and are different aspects about what happens when a person is "born again" and becomes "a child of God". They explain what really happens inside a true believer.

196. How can one show one's love for the Lord Jesus?

A. Read verses 21 and 23. See also question 188 and its answer. Note John 14:15 also. Note the priorities in John's Gospel. Keeping the commandments, obeying teaching, doing good deeds, etc., does not earn people eternal life. Eternal life is given freely, by God, to those who have faith in the manifestation of Himself in the Lord Jesus Christ but ... when one has faith and trust in the Lord Jesus and love starts to grow, then, if that faith is true faith, it will manifest itself in the desire to obey His teaching.

197. What was the Counsellor, the Holy Spirit, to do for the disciples?
A. Read verse 26.

198. Who is the "Prince of this World" and does he have any effect on the Lord Jesus?

A. The prince, ruler, of the world is Satan and he had no effect upon the Lord Jesus Christ, verse 30. The fact is that there is no sin in the Lord Jesus for Satan to work upon. See the answers to questions 20 and 123.

ANSWERS WITH QUESTIONS: CHAPTER 15

199. Who is the vine and who is the gardener

A. Verse 1 states: "I am the true vine and my Father is the gardener".

Verse 5 states: "I am the vine, you are the branches" and we see these statements are addressed to the disciples. Thus the fine and its branches is an illustration of the Lord Jesus and His disciples. The disciples would be familiar with this illustration of a vine and would appreciate the point the Lord Jesus made about bearing fruit or being a failure.

The gardener has two jobs to do on a vine:

a) The branches that bear no fruit are cut off, John 15:2, but this would only be after much care had been given to them. These fruitless branches would first be cared for by raising them so that extra air and sunlight may stimulate them.

b) Attention must be given to the branches that do bear fruit. "While every branch that does bear fruit he trims clean so that it will be even more fruitful", John 15:2. This involves pruning and its result is a cleansing.

The Lord Jesus said to the remaining eleven, "you are already clean because of the word I have spoken to you". However, He had previously indicated that one of them was not clean, John 13:10 and 11 and these verses in John 15 must be read in the light of John 13. So it is that some point out that John 15:6 should read, "If anyone does not receive me, he is like *the* branch that is thrown away and withers, such branches are picked up, thrown into the fire and burned". The "the" here refers especially to Judas who crossed the line which divided the followers of light from the followers of darkness and as such it would be impossible for him to bear fruit. Such a branch is past helping, it must be cut off and is fit for only destruction, the fire. This *may* be an allusion to the Lake of Fire, Revelation 20:11-15, which is the Second Death and may indicate that Judas will have no place in the resurrection to eternal life.

200. Why should we be careful to abide in Christ?
A. The previous answer gives the *interpretation* of the opening verses but we can make some *applications* to ourselves. Verses 1-8 supply two positive reasons why believers should be careful to abide in the Lord Jesus.

Verse 4, "No branch can bear fruit by itself; it must remain in the vine. Neither can you bear fruit unless you remain in me".

Verse 5, "If a man remains in me and I in him, he will bear much fruit; apart from me you can do nothing".

The figure of bearing fruit implies a process of growth resulting in full maturity by which a plant bears fruit which contain seed. The plant can thus bring forth others like itself. This is how the believer should be – first a seed which starts to grow and when maturity is reached, he can help others get to know the Lord Jesus Christ – i.e. he has borne fruit. A believer can also bear the "Fruit of the Spirit", which Galatians 5:22 says is "love, joy, peace, patience, kindness, goodness, faithfulness, gentleness and self-control". Whichever fruit the Lord Jesus had in mind, neither can be obtained unless one abides in Him.

The statement "apart from me you can do nothing" may perplex a person who has not known the Lord Jesus for very long or has known Him only superficially, but many older folk will testify that the older they get and the more they know Him, the more they depend upon Him. None-the-less, one must remember the context of these words and note it is not dealing with the things of this world but dealing with something spiritual – i.e. either bringing others to know the Lord Jesus or acquiring the fruit of the Spirit. One may cope with the things of this world without abiding in Him but will one be able to help others spiritually or grow spiritually oneself without His help? One further point. Note from verse 16 how the Lord Jesus wants "fruit that will last".

201. What is the greatest love a person can have?
  A. Verse 13, "No one has greater love than the one who lays down his life for his friends".

However, God's love is even greater as He died for those who were His enemies. Romans 5:7-10, "Very rarely will anyone die for a righteous man, though for a good man someone may possibly dare to die. But God demonstrates his own love for us in this: While we were still sinners, Christ died for us. Since we have now been justified by his blood, how much more shall we be saved from God's wrath through him! For if, when we were God's enemies, we were reconciled through the death of his son, how much more, having been reconciled shall we be saved through his life!"

202. Did the disciples choose the Lord Jesus?
  A. Verse 16 states that they did not choose Him but that He, in fact, chose them. It was the custom of the Jews, at that time, to choose the Master or teacher they wanted to follow. Here we see the Lord Jesus reversed that custom.

If the words "The Father will give you whatever you ask in my name", verse 16, or the words "ask whatever you wish, and it will be given you" cause concern please see answer 194.

203. Why does the world hate believers in the Lord Jesus?
   A. This world hates believers because it first hated the Lord Jesus, verse 18. Believers do not belong to this world, verse 19, but just as the world persecuted the Lord Jesus, so it will persecute His followers, verse 20. "They will treat you this way because of my name, for they do not know the one who sent me".

204. Did the Jews have any excuse for their sin?
   A. Verse 22 states -
   "they have no excuse for their sin". But what sin is verses 22-24 concerned about?

   Verse 22, "If I had not come and spoken to them, they would not be guilty of sin". Thus, this sin has something to do with the people, their relationship with the Lord Jesus and His teaching.

   Verse 24, "If I had not done among them what no one else did, they would not be guilty of sin. But now they have seen these miracles …"

   The miraculous signs the Lord Jesus performed were those which the Messiah, the Christ, was prophesied to do. Yet the people still rejected Him and the sin these verses is concerned about is the one of their rejection of the Lord Jesus as the Messiah.

   If He hadn't come, they could not have rejected Him and thus would not have been guilty.

   If He had not performed the confirming miracles prophesied in the Old Testament, they would have had an excuse but He came and worked these miracles. They chose to ignore both what He said and what He did and they rejected Him – so they had "no excuse for their sin".

205. Why did the world hate the Lord Jesus?
   They had no reason. Read verses 22-25.

206. What will the Holy Spirit, the Spirit of truth, do?
   A. He will testify about the Lord Jesus, verse 26. See also John 14:26.

207. Who else must testify?

    A. The disciples, verse 27.

208. Why must these testify?
    A. Verse 27,
    "… you also must testify, for you have been with me from the beginning".

This is an important point and has some bearing upon Judas' replacement. In Acts 1:21 and 22 Peter says, "Therefore it is necessary to choose one of the men who have been with us the whole time the Lord Jesus went in and out among us, beginning from John's baptism to the time when Jesus was taken up from us. For one of these must become a witness with us of his resurrection".

There were two who fulfilled the conditions Peter mentioned in the words of John 15:27. These were Justus and Matthias and the latter was chosen. Paul never saw the Lord Jesus in the flesh and certainly was not with Him from the beginning and could not satisfy the criterion required of the twelve apostles who were to be the leaders of the movement to make known the gospel to the Jews. God had another work for Paul – namely taking the gospel to the Gentiles.

ANSWERS WITH QUESTIONS: CHAPTER 16

209. What is to happen to the disciples?
    A. Read verses 2 and 3.
    We still have misguided persecution with us today and there is a danger that some will blame God for men's stupidity. In verse 2 we see true followers of God being cast out of the religious establishment. This has happened all through history and does it still happen today? It probably does and in the eyes of the non-committed onlooker it brings shame on the name of the Lord Jesus Christ. We may well disagree with people and hold different beliefs but we should still care about them. If we are to love our enemies, people with great differences from ourselves, how much more should we love those with whom we have much smaller differences.

210. Why was it necessary for the Lord Jesus to go away?
    A. Read verse 7.

211. What was to be the work of the Counsellor, the Holy Spirit, when He came?

A. Read verses 8-11.

Note that the manifestations of the Holy Spirit in the miraculous signs of the Acts period is not spoken of here. These verses give us the perpetual work of the Spirit; His special work of the Acts period was for a time only.

The perpetual work of the Holy Spirit, summarized in verse 8, is to prove the world wrong in three things:

SIN, verse 9
In God's sight sin is the refusal to believe Him and in particular not to believe in His Son, the Lord Jesus Christ; see also 1 John 5:10. This was *the* sin the Jews were guilty of at that time and the one dealt with in John 15:22-24. The Jews regarded only moral offences or breaking of the ceremonial law or a breaking of the traditions of the elders (Matthew 15:12) as sin. Today amongst some people, not even a breaking of the laws of parliament are considered a sin.

RIGHTEOUSNESS, verse 10
Again there is a difference between God's standard and man's. The Jews regarded the Pharisees with their great attention to formalities, (Luke 18:11,12), as their ideal. But the true standard required meticulous attention to carrying out God's will. The Lord Jesus Christ did just that (John 8:29) and was truly righteous but was rejected and crucified. However, in righteousness, or justification, He was resurrected from the dead and ascended from the earth to the right hand of God. He kept the standard; we cannot, but "in the gospel a righteousness from God is revealed, *a righteousness that is by faith* from first to last, just as it is written 'the righteous will live by faith'" (Romans 1:17). Thus faith in the Lord Jesus is what justifies us, is what makes us righteous.

JUDGMENT, verse 11
The prince of this world, Satan, has already been judged, (John 12:31). He has been sentenced and one day that sentence will be carried out.

212. Of whom was the Spirit of truth to speak?

A. Read verses 13-15 and note also John 15:26.

There are some organisations and institutions which speak much of the Holy Spirit. We have seen how the Scriptures can be abused and not give life because those who read them do not turn to the Lord Jesus – John 5:39, 40 and see the answers to questions 83 and 84. Similarly here, using the Holy Spirit's name means nothing. His job is to testify about and bring glory to the Lord Jesus Christ. Institutions which have much testimony about and give glory to the Holy Spirit apart from Christ need to be careful. What may be influencing them is not God, the Holy Spirit, but another – the prince of this world – John 16:11.

The Lord Jesus said the prince of this world was coming, John 14:30, and will one day be driven out, John 12:31, but in the meantime he is doing his best to confuse and deceive. This possibly accounts for much misunderstanding and disagreement amongst believers which brings shame on the name Christian. (See also the answer to question 209).

213. Did the disciples understand what the Lord Jesus was referring to in verse 16?
    A. No – read verses 17 and 18.
What does the Lord Jesus mean in verse 16?

214. What is the Lord Jesus referring to in verse 20?
    A. When the Lord Jesus was crucified, His disciples mourned but when He came back to life their grief was turned to joy which no one could take away. See also verse 22.

215. When will the disciples be able to ask anything in the Lord's name and have it come to pass?
    A. Verse 23 – "In that day …"
    Verse 26 – "In that day …"

"That day" is an expression which has occurred a number of times. For example in John 14:20 we read, "On that day you will realise that I am in my Father, and you are in me, and I am in you".

Here, "on that day" refers primarily to the forty days after His resurrection but the phrase "on that day" was a well-known saying used to describe "the day of the Lord" – a period of time associated with Christ's second coming.

Again, John 16:23 states, "In that day you will no longer ask me anything. I tell you the truth, My Father will give you whatever you ask in my name".

The disciples were able to ask anything in the Lord's name not only during the 40-day period after His resurrection but also throughout the subsequent Acts period. However, when He returns the second time and the disciples are raised to eternal life, they will again be able to ask.

Some, in this age, do sincerely ask in His name and as far as they can see, in harmony with His will, yet nothing appears to happen. This has led to the weakening of the faith of some, and really the problem is caused by taking passages of the Scripture out of context and so misunderstanding the will of God. Not only out of the context of what is written immediately before and after them but also they have taken them out of the context of time, person and purpose – i.e. when it was written, to whom it was written and why it was written. Centuries ago Miles Coverdale gave this advice:

"It shall greatly helpe ye to understand Scripture
if thou mark,
not only what is spoken, or wrytten,,
but of whom,
and to whom,
with what words,
at what time,
where,
to what intent,
with what circumstances,
considering what goeth before and what followeth".

With those words we cannot disagree.

216. Why did the Father love them?
    A. Read verse 27.

In John 3:16 we see an expression of God's love to the world. Here we see a further expression to those who love the Lord Jesus and believe He came from God.

217. Did the disciples understand the Lord Jesus when He no longer used figures of speech?

A. Read verses 29, 30.

218. Did they believe He came from God?

A. Yes – verse 30, which also indicates their reason for doing so. They believe because of His deep understanding of them, their thoughts, their questions, their motives. We read earlier – John 2:25 – that "he knew what was in a man" and in John 1:42 and 1:47 and 48 we see He knew all about His followers even before He met them. In John 16:17-18 He knew what question was on their mind. They didn't ask it but He approached them (see also Mark 9:32-34 and Luke 9:44-47). This must have impressed them, for they said, "you don't even need to have anyone ask you questions" – John 16:30.

219. Where could the disciples find peace and why?

A. Verse 33. In the Lord Jesus, because He had overcome the world.

See also John 14:27 – "Peace I leave with you; my peace I give you. I do not give to you as the world gives. Do not let your hearts be troubled and do not be afraid".

ANSWERS WITH QUESTIONS: CHAPTER 17

220. What is life eternal?

A. Verse 3 –

"Now this is life eternal: that men may know you, the only true God, and Jesus Christ, whom you have sent".

Now this is not really a definition of life eternal but more a description of the purpose for which it is given. That men will know the only true God: that men will acquire knowledge about the only true God; that men will become acquainted with the only true God. We shall have full knowledge and become fully acquainted with Him when we have been raised from the dead and have eternal life but we have already started acquiring knowledge of the only true God. This is what the reader is now doing, and rightly so. Until one has a measure of knowledge about God, we cannot represent Him truly or tell others about Him. Thus knowledge of God is important.

221. Read carefully the Lord's prayer for His disciples.
   A. Read verses 6-19.
   In verse 13 the Lord stated, "I say these things while I am still in the world, so that they (the disciples) may have the full measure of my joy within them". Why saying these things before His resurrection ensures the full measure of His joy may be difficult to ascertain. No doubt, many things He said to them before His death acquired far greater depth of meaning after His resurrection and undoubtedly increased their faith, and thus their joy. See obvious examples in John 2:18-22 and John 12:12-16.

222. Did the disciples accept the word of the Lord Jesus?
   A. Verses 7 and 8 –
   "They know now that everything you have given me comes from you. For I gave them the words you gave me and they accepted them. They know with certainty that I come from you, and they believed that you sent me".

   Yes – they knew with certainty but today many are far from certain and do lack assurance. Perhaps they have failed to get to know the only true God and have not realised the purpose of life eternal is to enable man to get to know the only true Go, verse 3. Naturally, lack of knowledge will bring lack of assurance and lack of certainty. Failure, not only in understanding the Bible but also in reading it, must produce even greater ignorance of God.

223. Who is the child of hell (literally "son of perdition")?
   A. In verse 12 the Lord Jesus claims responsibility for the protection and safeguarding of the eleven and He indicates the power of His name to keep people. Verse 11 states this is also the Father's name and the Father gave it to the Son. Here we see the unique oneness between them but which of the many names or titles of the Lord Jesus is meant here is not indicated.

   The "child of hell" is Judas and an alternative translation is "son of perdition". This title is a description of his character which indicates that he had completely gone over to the way which must end in total loss.

The Scripture which was to be fulfilled could be Psalm 41:9, which is quoted in John 13:18 and fulfilled in John 13:26, 27. (See also answer 185).

224. Did He want His disciples taken out of this world?
    A. No – verse 15.

225. Read carefully the Lord's prayer for all believers.
    A. Read verses 20-26.
Note that verse 23 indicates that the Father loves all believers as much as His own Son.

226. Why did the Lord Jesus want all believers to be a complete unity?
    A. Verse 23 –
"May they be brought to a complete unity to let the world know that you sent me and have loved them even as you have loved me".

There is a great urge for Church Unity today but is the purpose of it the same as that stated by the Lord Jesus? Will a change of name or a compromise over doctrine make the churches upon this earth any more of a unity in the eyes of God? Do we need a secular organisational unity when Scripture talks about a Spiritual unity that already exists and which we are told to keep (Ephesians 4:3)? To keep this unity, what we have to do is to "love one another" and guard the truth which has been committed to us. "All men will know you are my disciples if you love one another", John 13:34, 35.

This is true unity and makes the unifying efforts of organisations a very poor second best.

227. How do we get to know the Father?
    A. Read verses 25 and 26.
We get to know the Father through the Son who is revealed in the written word which the Holy Spirit, the author, will reveal to believers. (See answer 220).

ANSWERS WITH QUESTIONS: CHAPTER 18

228. What happened to the soldiers and the officers when the Lord Jesus gave His title "I AM"?

A. Verse 6 –
"They drew back and fell on the ground". Now why did they do this? Let us read verses 4-6 again.

"Who is it you want?"
"Jesus of Nazareth", they replied.
"I AM", Jesus said. (And Judas the traitor was standing there with them). When Jesus said, "I AM", they drew back and fell to the ground.

The "he" of verses 5 and 6 are not in the original Greek and have been put in by the translators to ensure the English makes sense, but more sense of the situation is made if they are left out. Here the Lord Jesus is again using God's exclusive name of Himself. (See John 8:58 and answer 125). It was the Lord Jesus' claim to God's name and the power of His deity that caused them to draw back and fall to the ground and He explained this in verse 8 when He said, "I told you that I AM".

229. What did Peter do?

A. See verse 10, where we have another example of Peter being impetuous – see answer 179.

It might be a surprise to some to find Peter carrying a sword but please read Luke 22:35-38. In verse 35 the Lord Jesus says "when I sent you without purse, bag or sandals, did you lack anything?"

Here He is referring back to Luke 9:2-5 where the twelve were sent to "preach the kingdom of God" but many did not accept this testimony. They did not listen to the twelve or to the Lord Jesus; thus in Luke 22:36 He says "*But NOW* if you have a purse take it, and also a bag, and if you don't have a sword, sell your cloak and buy one". Thus in Luke 22:35-38 we see different teaching from that in Luke 9:2-5. This is because the instructions given when the kingdom of God was being preached and accepted were no longer suitable when that message was being rejected.

230. Did the Lord Jesus resist arrest?

A. No – verses 7-11. A little earlier, John 17:1, the Lord Jesus said "the hour is come". He had come to die on the cross and the time was now right. On earlier occasions we see that His enemies could not touch Him; see John 7:30; 8:20 and answer 102.

231. What did the Lord Jesus mean when He said, "Shall I not drink the cup the Father has given me?"?

A. The cup the Lord Jesus is referring to is His death on the cross. The question, which was addressed to Peter, must be answered with a resounding "Yes".

In John 12:27 the Lord Jesus says "Now my heart is troubled and what shall I say" 'Father, save me from this hour'? No it was for this very reason I came to this hour". (See answer 164).

Thus the question "Shall I not drink the cup the Father has given me?" has been answered earlier with the statement "It was for this very reason I came to this hour". See also the following verses:

John 10:11 – "I am the good shepherd. The good shepherd lays down his life for the sheep".

John 10:13 – "… I lay down my life – only to take it up again".

John 10:18 – "No one takes it from me, but I lay it down of my own accord. I have authority to lay it down and authority to take it up again".

John 12:24 – "… unless a kernel of wheat falls to the ground and dies, it remains only a single seed. But if it dies, it produces many seeds".

John 12:32 – "But when I am lifted up from the earth, I will draw all men to myself. He said this to show the kind of death He was going to die"

Thus from these few verses alone we see that the Lord Jesus was more than willing to drink of the cup of death on the cross.

But what about Luke 22:42 – "Father, if you are willing, take this cup from me; yet not my will, but yours, be done".

Read Luke 22:39-46. There the Lord Jesus was in the garden and on the point of death – verse 44 – and He required strengthening – verse 43. It was the cup of death in the garden that He did not want to drink, because He wanted to drink from the other cup, the cup of death on the cross.

In the garden Satan was trying to thwart God's plan by causing the premature death of the Lord Jesus but He was strengthened and live to die at the right time and in a way that had been chosen and recorded in the Old Testament. Galatians 3:13, "Cursed is everyone who is hanged on a tree", is a quotation from Deuteronomy 21:23. (See answer 102).

232. When had Caiaphas advised the Jews that it would be best if one man died for the people?
A. Read John 11:49, 50 and the answer to question 155.

Perhaps the reader had difficulty in finding this previous verse. We all have that trouble and for those with a poor memory, perhaps the following suggestions may be of help:

(a) It is quite all right to mark your Bible but perhaps, first of all, it is best to use pencil – it is easier to rub out. You may wish to underline certain verses or put marks by the side of them. You may want to write certain cross references in the margin or to add explanatory notes of your own There are certain Bibles – e.g. the Oxford Wide Margin edition of the Authorized Version – which are especially designed for this.

(b) A concordance is a book which has an alphabetical arrangement of the chief words or subjects of another book. There are concordances of the Bible which make it easy to find any verse – e.g. *Young's Analytical Concordance* or *Strong's Exhaustive Concordance.*

233. What does the Lord Jesus say about His teaching?
A. In verse 20 He says -
"I have always taught in synagogues or at the temple, where all the Jews come together". (See answer 180).

234. Did Peter prove the Lord Jesus right?

A. Read John 13:38 and compare it with John 18:17-27.

Yes – Peter did prove the Lord Jesus right but don't be too harsh on him. Only he and John (see 19:26) stayed anywhere near the Lord Jesus during this difficult time. The others were nowhere in the vicinity, as far as we know.

It is difficult to say who the other disciple mentioned in 18:15 and 16 is, but it is probably John.

235. Why did the Jews not judge the Lord Jesus themselves?

A. They wanted to have Him executed – verse 31. However, for violations of their law, they seem to have had the power of stoning to death (John 8:59 and 10:31, Acts 7:59). Thus, they could have stoned Him but no doubt they feared the people and so decided to raise the plea of rebellion against Caesar. Perhaps they wanted to put the blame for the Lord's death upon Pilate, but if we compare John 18:32 with John 12:33 we see the Lord Jesus clearly indicated what kind of death He was to suffer. Thus, even though the Jews were held responsible for His death (see later question 242), He was not executed by their method of stoning but was executed in the Roman fashion.

236. Was the Lord's kingdom of this world?

A. No – verse 36.

The words of the Lord's Prayer "Thy kingdom come, thy will be done on earth as it is in heaven" may add some light on what the Lord Jesus is saying. His kingdom does not originate from earth but from heaven and one day the words of that prayer will be fulfilled – but not until the Lord Jesus returns.

237. Did the Lord Jesus answer the question "Are you the king of the Jews?"?

A. In verse 33 Pilate asked, "Are you the king of the Jews?" and the Lord Jesus does not answer him at first. He asks Pilate a question – verse 34 – and after further conversation Pilate says in verse 37, "You are a king then!" to which the Lord Jesus answers "You are right in saying I am a king".

Please note the Lord's answers in Matthew 27:11, Mark 15:2, Luke 22:70, 23:3. The AV translation gives "Thou sayest it" as His answer but the NIV has, "Yes, it is as you say", and this is better. "Thou sayest it" has been understood by some as an evasive answer on the part of the Lord Jesus but it is in fact a figure of speech denoting *strong agreement* with what has just been said. We use a similar expression to denote agreement in this day and age – "you've said it".

238. What was Pilate's opinion after he had examined the Lord Jesus?
   A. "I find no basis for a charge against him", verse 38. See answers 20, 123 and 198.

239. Did the people want the Lord Jesus to be freed?
   A. No. They wanted Barabbas to be freed – verse 40.

ANSWERS WITH QUESTIONS: CHAPTER 19

240. How was the Lord Jesus treated by the soldiers?
   A. Read verses 1-3.

241. Did Pilate find the Lord Jesus guilty of anything at all?
   A. No – read verses 4-6. See also answers 20, 123, 198 and 238.

242. Was Pilate to bear the responsibility of the Lord's death?
   A. In verses 1-16 we see how Pilate tried to free the Lord Jesus (verses 4, 6 and 12) but he didn't because he was afraid (verse 8), and what the Jews were saying (verses 12 and 16) must have caused him concern. But he was not held responsible for the death of the Lord Jesus. Read verse 11 where it says, "The one who handed me over to you is guilty of a greater sin".

   Now this does *not* refer to Judas, who had delivered the Lord Jesus to the Sanhedrin, the ruling council of the Jews, but to the leader of that council, Caiaphas, who had delivered Him to Pilate. Thus it is that the responsibility for His death was upon the shoulders of the Jewish nation and in Acts 5:30 Peter says to the Jews, "The God of our fathers raised Jesus from the dead – whom *you* killed by hanging on a tree". And in Acts 10:39 Peter says about the Jews, "They killed him by hanging him on a tree".

   Thus it was this nation which committed the great sin but on the cross the Lord Jesus said in Luke 23:23, "Father, forgive them for they know not what they are doing" and this prayer cannot refer to the Roman soldiers, because the blame had not been put upon their shoulders. It was a prayer for that Jewish nation and it was answered. That nation was forgiven and was given another chance to repent of their ways and accept the Lord Jesus as their Messiah. Just as the Lord Jesus had called upon them to repentance during His earthly ministry, so Peter and the twelve made the call for repentance during the Acts period. Acts 2:38, "Peter replied, 'Repent and be baptised, every one of you in the name of the Lord Jesus'". Also, Acts 3:19, "Repent, then, and turn to God, so that your sins may be wiped out, that the times of refreshing may come from the Lord, and that he may send the Christ, who has been appointed for you – even Jesus".

If that nation had repented, the Lord Jesus would have returned. But they did not, and because of their continued failure to repent and accept the Lord Jesus they were set aside at the end of the Acts period. We then have a new revelation from God called the revelation of the Mystery, which is set forth from the end of the Acts period by the apostle Paul in Ephesians, Philippians, Colossians, Philemon, 1 and 2 Timothy and Titus. However, we cannot say that God has completely finished with the Jewish nation. He made promises to their forefathers which have not yet been fulfilled and one day, maybe not very far in the future, He will start to work with them again.

243. What seven questions did Pilate ask the Lord Jesus?
(Four are in chapter 18).

A. 18:33 – "Are you the king of the Jews?"
18:35 – "What is it you have done?"
18:37 – "You are a king then!"
18:38 – "What is truth?"
19: 9 – "Where do you come from?"
19:10 – "Do you refuse to speak to me?"
19:10 – "Don't you realise I have power either to free you or crucify you?"

These were Pilate's seven questions and the fifth one may have expressed something stirring within him. Pilate was possibly a deep thinker, as some infer from the question "What is truth?" But this question may just show he was somewhat tired of the various philosophies and religions which contended for acceptance.

244. Where was the Lord Jesus to be executed?
   A. Golgotha – verse 17.

245. What title did Pilate write on the cross?
   A. "Jesus of Nazareth, the King of the Jews"-verse 19.

246. What prophecy was next fulfilled?
   A. Verse 24 sees the fulfillment of another prophecy given in Psalm 22:18.

   Verse 29 is a fulfillment of Psalm 69:21. There are many prophecies related to the crucifixion and we cannot give details of them all but to read the whole of Psalm 22 would be beneficial.

247. What women were present at the scene?
   A. "His mother, his mother's sister, Mary the wife of Clopas, and Mary of Magdala" – verse 25.

248. Who was the disciple the Lord Jesus loved and what did He ask him to do?
   A. "The disciple whom he loved" refers to John (see 21:20-24), the writer of the Gospel, and He asked him to look after Mary – verses 26, 27. Joseph was evidently dead and as none of His brothers at this time believed in Him John 7:3-5, it seems fitting that one of His followers should do it.

249. What were the last words uttered by the Lord Jesus on the cross?
   A. There were seven recorded sayings on the cross by the Lord Jesus and we suggest a careful reading of Matthew 27:33-50, Mark 15:22-39, Luke 23:33-47 and John 19:17-30. The order of these sayings are:

   (a) Luke 23:34 "Father, forgive them, for they do not know what they are doing".

   (b) Luke 23:43 "I tell you the truth today, you will be with me in paradise".

   (c) John 19:26 and 19:27 " Here is your son".

   (d) Matthew 27:46 and Mark 15:34 "My God, my God, why have you forsaken me?"

(e) John 19:28 "I am thirsty".

(f) John 19:30 "It is finished".

(g) Luke 23:46 "Father, into your hands I commit my spirit".

We see that one saying is recorded twice – "My God, my God, why have you forsaken me" - (Matthew 27:46; Mark 15:34). It is very difficult to know or understand what really went on here. Some state that this verse shows that the Lord Jesus Christ was not God and here God deserted Him. We see this would run contrary to what we have so far read of John's writing and we should not disbelieve just because we cannot fully understand some aspect of God. We may have some little insight into what happened from other parts of Scripture.

We often mention how the Lord Jesus died for our sins and this was possible because He fulfilled the sin-offering sacrifice of the Old Testament. This was possible because, as 2 Corinthians 5:21 puts it, "God made him who had no sin to be sin for us, so that in him we might be the righteousness of God". In many ways this was the real misery of the cross. Death was bad enough, but to be made sin must have added much to the suffering and misery and it was the adding of sin that caused the words "My God, my God, why have you forsaken me" to be uttered.

We have already seen that it is impossible to understand the person of the Lord Jesus Christ. He is Man but He is also God, but can the finite ever comprehend and understand the infinite? No. So we ask, can we understand what really happened on the cross when "God made him who had no sin to be sin for us"? Nonetheless, by faith we can be sure of these two things. We can be sure that the Lord Jesus Christ is God and on the cross He became sin for us. How these are possible is beyond us but one day we shall know, the day when we are with Him.

However, whatever it was that happened – it was over, within hours, when the Lord Jesus said, "It is finished". These words refer to the glorious redemptive work which He came to do in bearing the sins of His people. Shortly after this He said, "Father, into your hands I commit my Spirit", which were His final words till after His resurrection.

For comments on the expression "Father, forgive them for they do not know what they are doing", see answer 242.

The reader will note that we have changed the punctuation of "I tell you the truth, today you will be with me in paradise", to "I tell you the truth today, you will be with me in paradise". Greek manuscripts have no punctuation and when translating it is a matter of opinion how to punctuate the English. However, we know that eternal life will not be started until "the resurrection at the last day" – John 11:24 – so it seems strange to tell the criminal that "today" it will start. We know that David, who slew Goliath and became the nation's greatest king, was still in the grave and had not ascended to heaven – Acts 2:29-34. Thus it seems strange to tell the criminal that "today" was his time. We know that the Lord Jesus Christ spent the rest of that day and the following two in the grave. He did not go to paradise that day and so could not have said "today you will be *with me* in paradise" because He wasn't there Himself. But the Lord Jesus did tell the criminal that he would be with Him in paradise – and the start of that life there would be on the day of resurrection.

The problem is another figure of speech. We have a similar one which we use today. It varies throughout the country but could be something like "I'm telling you now, I'm going out". It doesn't say when the person is going out and we would have to ascertain that from more of the conversation. We misrepresent what the Lord Jesus said when we fail to recognise the well-used figure of speech of His day, "I tell you the truth today ..." If we change the punctuation, we give it a completely different meaning and a wrong one. From what He said to the criminal, we cannot ascertain when paradise would be entered. We need to either know more of the conversation or more of what the Lord Jesus taught.

250. When did the Lord Jesus die on the cross?
   A. From verse 31 we see that it was the day of Preparation, the day before the Sabbath (see also verse 14).

251. Why did the soldiers not break His legs?
   A. "He was already dead" – verse 33. Read verses 31-37.

Note verse 36 is a fulfillment of prophecies in Exodus 12:46, Numbers 9:12 and Psalm 34:20. Verse 37 is a fulfillment of Zechariah 12:10.

252. Who helped Joseph of Arimathea with the body of the Lord Jesus?
   A. Verse 39 – it was Nicodemus.
   See John 3:1-21 and 7:45-52 and answers to 44, 110 and 234.

ANSWERS WITH QUESTIONS: CHAPTER 20

253. What did Mary say when she found the tomb empty?
Read verse 2.
   A. Unfortunately she was not looking for or expecting His resurrection in spite of all the Lord Jesus had said. Note "the other disciple" in verses 2, 3, 4 and 8. Here John is again referring to himself.

254. What did the Lord Jesus have to do?
   A. Read verses 6-9.
   "Jesus had to rise from the dead".

255. Did the other disciple see and believe?
   A. Yes – verse 8.
   He believed the Lord Jesus had risen. Much of what the Lord Jesus had said to His disciples about rising again the third day was not understood and not believed by them, yet the Pharisees had taken note – see Matthew 27:63.

256. What was Mary's reply to the angel?
   A. Read verse 13.
   She still did not realise He had risen from the dead. Mary saw two angels in white and from Luke 24:4 these same beings are described as "two men in clothes that gleamed like lightning". There is no mention of halos or wings. "Some people have entertained angels without knowing it", Hebrews 13:2. One is unlikely to do that if they have great big wings etc.!! I am afraid that artists' impressions of angels and how they appear are just not scriptural. Read Genesis 18 and 19 to see how they appeared to an ordinary man and how they did also eat a meal.

257. What was Mary's reply to the Lord Jesus?

A. Verse 15 – "Thinking he was the gardener, she said, 'Sir, if you have carried him away, tell me where you have put him, and I will get him'".

Verse 16 – "Jesus said to her, 'Mary'. She turned toward him and cried in Aramaic, 'Rabboni!' (which means teacher)".

258. Could the disciples forgive sins?
A. At a first reading it looks as if verse 23 means that the disciples could forgive the sins of anyone they chose. This would be diametrically against the rest of Scripture which deals with the forgiveness of sins – i.e. the need for faith in Christ as the Sin bearer and Saviour.

Note that there is not one record in the Bible of any of the apostles using this command of John 20:23 in this way. Therefore it can only mean that by the faithful preaching of the Gospel they would bring their hearers to a decision which would decide whether they would be forgiven or not. Thus the apostles could say that those who believed in this way could be forgiven and those who did not believe would not be forgiven.

259. What was Thomas' comment when the others told him that they had seen the Lord Jesus?
A. Verse 25 –
"Unless I see the nail marks in his hands and put my finger where the nails were, and put my hand into his side, I will not believe it".

260. What was Thomas' statement when he himself saw the Lord Jesus?
Verse 28 –
A. "My Lord and my God".

And this is what the Lord Jesus Christ should be to each and every one who claims to follow Him. Both Lord and God.

261. What was the reply the Lord Jesus made to that statement?
Verse 29 –
A. "Because you have seen me, you have believed; blessed are those who have not seen, yet have believed".

262. Why did John write his gospel?

A. Note the words of verse 30.

John chose the material for his writing with the purpose "that you may believe that Jesus is the Christ, the Son of God, and that believing you may have life through his name" verse 31.

This can be taken not only as the purpose of John's gospel but also as the main purpose of the Bible. The Bible sets forth God's plan of redemption – i.e. how man's sins can be forgiven and how he can gain access to God and have eternal life. It is on questions pertaining to this that the Bible gives the answers. The Bible is not a textbook of how God created; it is not merely a history book or a book to tell us of the future. True, aspects of these and other subjects may come into the Bible but the Bible is a book which tells us about the working of our Great God and Saviour, Jesus Christ.

ANSWERS WITH QUESTIONS: CHAPTER 21

263. Did they realise it was the Lord Jesus talking to them?
   A. No – verse 4,
   yet they had known Him earlier – John 20:26-29. Mary didn't realise it was Him in John 20:14 and 15 and on the road to Emmaus – Luke 24:13-35 – two of them didn't realise it was Him for quite some time. Is there something different about the resurrection body? From these verses and John 20:26 it would seem that there was!

264. Who said to Peter "It is the Lord"?
   A. Read verse 7.

265. Did the disciples know it was the Lord Jesus?
   A. Yes – verse 12.
   Note that "None of the disciples dares ask him, 'Who are you'" Before His resurrection they questioned Him freely, but it appears that this great event brought about a change in their relationship with Him. They now had a greater understanding of the One they were following.

   Notice the change in Thomas' comments in John 20 and compare verses 25 and 28.

Notice the impetuous Peter seems very subdued in John 21:15 and 19.

266. How many times had the Lord Jesus appeared to His disciples after His death?
A. Up to then, three times –
verse 14, but there were more.

267. What three questions did the Lord Jesus ask Peter?
A. Verse 15 – "Simon son of John, do you truly love me more than these?"
Verse 16 – "Simon son of John, do you truly love me?"
Verse 17 – "Simon son of John, do you love me?"

Note how Peter would not say that he "truly loved" the Lord Jesus. No doubt he did, but after his denials he was not prepared to say so. Perhaps he was still ashamed; we do not know. However, note that the Lord Jesus shows him that love must be translated into actions.

268. What four instructions did He give Peter
A. Verse 15 – "Feed my lambs".
Verse 16 – "Take care of my sheep".
Verse 17 – "Feed my sheep".
Verse 19 – "Follow me!".

269. The Lord Jesus indicated what death Peter would suffer but did this deter Peter from following Him?
A. No – The expression "you will stretch out your hand" probably refers to crucifixion.

270. How do we know that the disciple often alluded to, but never mentioned, is John, the writer of this gospel?
A. Read verses 20-24.

271. Did the Lord Jesus do many other things?
A. Read John 20:3, 31 and 21:25.

It is correct to say that the Bible is "nothing but the truth" but it is not correct to say it is the complete record of all that man would like to know e.g. *how* did God create? Here John clearly says that it would be impossible to record all the activities of the Lord

Jesus, yet He ministered for only 3 ½ years. He must have been in similar situations many times and performed many deeds of a similar nature. Thus, in the Gospels, we get events recorded which may be the same but could easily be different and it is no proof that Matthew, Mark, Luke and John disagree because their description of a certain event is different. They may be referring to similar acts which took place at different times in different places. What they describe may be completely different events which have some things in common.

"Jesus did many other things as well. If every one of these were written down, I suppose that even the whole world would not have room for the books that would be written."

"But these are written that you may believe that Jesus is the Christ, the Son of God, and that believing you may have life through his name".

* * * * * * * *

Having completed our study of it, it would be a good idea to read right through John's Gospel again. This will be of great help and the reader will be surprised how much is recalled and how much has been learnt. If both the NIV and the AV have been obtained, this could be done twice. First read through the NIV translation of John, and then through the AV, or another translation. The reader should find this profitable and comparisons of different translations will always bring new points to the surface.

SECTION FOUR
Main Themes in John's Gospel

Having studied John's Gospel in the way that we have, there is a danger that it will be all "bits and pieces", and thus this section aims at pulling together some of the main themes that run through this gospel.

1. Witness in John's Gospel

We hear much about 'witnessing' in these days and the word to bear witness, marturea occurs 33 times in John - (once in Matthew, twice in Luke). The word for witness, marturia, occurs 14 times in John – (three times in Mark, once in Luke). We won't give the complete list, but point out that this witness was borne by:

1	the Father	5:22, 37; 8:18
2	the Son	8:14; 18:37
3	the Holy Spirit	15:26; 16:13, 14
4	the Written Word	1:45; 5:39, 46
5	the Works	5:17, 36; 10:25; 14:11; 15:24
6	John the Baptist	1:7; 5:33, 35
7	the Disciples	15:27; 19:35; 21:14

2. The Lord Jesus Christ in John's Gospel

We mentioned, in answer 23, that the many titles and descriptions of the Lord Jesus endeavour to show different aspects of His character and work; both being so great that it is impossible to describe either in simple terms. One purpose of John's Gospel is to present the Lord Jesus Christ as God, and this is the greatest difference between the first three Gospels and this one. In Matthew's Gospel we have the Lord Jesus presented as Israel's King, the King of the Jews. In Mark He is presented as God's servant. In Luke He is seen as the perfect Man and in John He is presented as God. Thus, each writer was inspired to select incidents, words and

Manual on the Gospel of John

work which most suited his presentation of the Lord Jesus. Matthew, Mark and Luke each present one aspect of the Perfect humanity of the Lord Jesus. This is what links them together and why the three of them together are called the synoptic Gospels, but it is also what distinguishes them from John's Gospel.

In John it is the person of the Lord Jesus that is presented rather than an aspect of His mission. The purpose in John is the presentation of the Lord Jesus as the Christ, the Messiah, and His deity is seen throughout the gospel. For example see:

> John 1:1, 3, 14, 33, 34, 49
> 3:13, 14
> 5:23, 26
> 6:51, 62
> 8:58
> 13:33

and there are more which the reader may care to find. The last reference is in John 20:31 but the most emphatic is just before that in John 20:28, when Thomas calls the Lord Jesus

> "My Lord and my God".

3. Life in John's Gospel

The main purpose of John's Gospel is summed up in his own words in John 20:30, 31.

"Jesus did many other miraculous signs in the presence of his disciples, which are not recorded in this book. But these are written that you may believe that Jesus is the Christ, the Son of God, and that by believing you may have LIFE in his name".

The Greek word for believe is pisteuo and occurs no less than 99 times in John's Gospel – (11 in Matthew, 15 in Mark and 9 in Luke). It is derived from pistis which is the word translated belief, faith, trust. So we see how these three are closely related. It is belief, faith, trust in the Lord Jesus Christ that gives life. The word for life is zoe and occurs 36 times in John – (7 in Matthew, 4 in Mark and 6 in Luke). The references are as follows:

	Life	(1:4)
Eternal	Life	(3:15,16,36)
	Life	(3:36)
Eternal	Life	(4:14,36; 5:24)
	Life	(5:24,26,29)
Eternal	Life	(5:39)
	Life	(5:40)
Eternal	Life	(6:27)
	Life	(6:33,35)
Eternal	Life	(6:40,47)
	Life	(6:48,51,53)
Eternal	Life	(6:54)
	Life	(6:63)
Eternal	Life	(6:68)
	Life	(8:12; 10:10)
Eternal	Life	(10:28)
	Life	(11:25; 12:25,25)
Eternal	Life	(12:25,50)
	Life	(14:6)
Eternal	Life	(17:2,3)
	Life	(20:31)

Note – eternal life and everlasting life are translations of the same Greek expression and obviously, even from the English, they must be the same.

Please read through each of the references and it will be seen that even when the word "life" is not prefixed by either "eternal" or "everlasting" it is usually referring to that future life. The word zoe is used of this present physical life in only one verse, 12:25, and then it is use to contrast it with eternal life. So we can see that eternal life is one of the main subjects of this gospel and the source of this eternal life is the Lord Jesus Christ.

John 1:4	In Him was LIFE
John 6:35	I am the bread of LIFE
John 11:25	I am the resurrection and the LIFE

How is this life obtainable?

| John 3:16 | Whoever believes in Him shall not perish but have everlasting LIFE |

| John 3:36 | Whoever puts his faith in the Son has eternal LIFE |
| John 5:24 | Whoever believes Him who sent me has eternal LIFE and will not be condemned; he has crossed over from death to LIFE |

All this may be summed up in just two verses from John's first epistle:

"…God has given us eternal LIFE, and this LIFE is in his Son. He who has the Son has LIFE: he who does not have the Son of God does not have LIFE" (1 John 5:11, 12).

4. The Miraculous signs in John's Gospel

In the Synoptic Gospels the Greek word used for miracles can be literally translated "mighty works" but this word does not occur in John's Gospel. He uses a word which should be translated "signs". John chooses to describe only eight signs because:

"Jesus did many other things as well. If every one of them were written down, I suppose that even the whole world would not have room for the books that would be written"
(John 21:25).

"… these are written that you may believe that Jesus is the Christ, the Son of God, and that by believing you may have life through his name".

Thus, these eight signs deserve a closer look. They are:

1.	The marriage in Cana	2:1-11
2.	The royal officer's son	4:43-52
3.	The invalid	5:1-15
4.	Feeding the five thousand	6:1-14
5.	Walking on the sea	6:15-21
6.	The man born blind	9:1-41
7.	Mary's brother, Lazarus	11:1-46
8.	The netful of fishes	21:1-14

We will say no more about these signs for the present. There is a close relationship between the first and the eighth, the second and the seventh, the third and the sixth, the fourth and the fifth, which the reader may care to look into for himself. If any have The Companion Bible, appendix 176 deals fully with these eight signs.

5. The I AM of John's Gospel

In answer 125 we dealt with the I AM statements of John 8:58 and John 8:24. We cannot give the details of all the occurrences of this expression but, as it forms a very distinctive feature of John's Gospel, we give the following outline, which the reader may care to look into.

The Messiah	I am He	4:26
Bread	I am the bread of life	6:35, 41, 48, 51
Light	I am the light of the world	8:12; 9:5
I AM	Before Abraham was born, I am	8:58 (8:24 answer 125,18:5, 6 answer 228)
Gate	I am the gate	10:7, 9
Shepherd	I am the good shepherd	10:11, 14
Life	I am the resurrection and the life	11:25
Way	I am the way – and the truth and the life	14:6
Vine	I am the true vine	15:1,5

6. "I tell you the truth" in John's Gospel

The Greek expression amen, amen occurs 25 times in John's Gospel, but not once in any of the others. It means literally "truth, truth" and is translated in the AV by "verily, verily" and in the NIV by "I tell you the truth". In John the use of this word twice is in order to depict, and thus emphasise, the greater words with which the Lord Jesus, as God, spoke. Thus we find it only in John's Gospel and these expressions come, if you like, with double the importance. We give the list and leave it to the reader to find for himself the greater details of those points the Lord Jesus called attention to by using this saying, "I tell you the truth":

1:51   You shall see heaven open, and the angels of God ascending and descending on the Son of Man.
3:3   Unless a man is born again, he cannot see the kingdom of God.

Manual on the Gospel of John

3:5	Unless a man is born of water and the Spirit, he cannot enter the kingdom of God.
3:11	We speak of what we know, and we testify of what we have seen, but still you people do not accept our testimony.
5:19	The Son can do nothing by himself; he can do only what he sees his Father doing, because whatever the Father does, the Son also does.
5:24	Whoever hears my words and believes him who sent me has eternal life and will not be condemned; he has crossed over from death to life.
5:25	A time is coming and has now come when the dead will hear the voice of the Son of God and those who hear will live.
6:26	You are looking for me, not because you saw miraculous signs but because you ate loaves and had your fill.
6:32	It is not Moses who has given you bread from heaven, but it is my Father who gives you the true bread from heaven.
6:47	He who believes has everlasting life.
6:53	Unless you eat the flesh of the Son of Man and drink his blood you have no life in you.
8:34	Everyone who sins is a slave to sin.
8:51	If a man keeps my word, he will never see death.
8:58	Before Abraham was, I am!
10:1	The man who does not enter the sheep-pen by the gate, but climbs in some other way, is a thief and a robber.
10:7	I am the gate for the sheep.
12:24	Unless a kernel of wheat falls to the ground and dies, it remains only a single seed. But, if it dies, it produces many seeds.
13:16	No servant is greater than his master, nor is a messenger greater than the one who sent him.
13:20	Whoever accepts anyone I send accepts me; and whoever accepts me, accepts the one who sent me.
13:21	One of you is going to betray me.
13:38	Before the cock crows, you will disown me three times!
14:12	Anyone who has faith in me will do what I have been doing. He will do even greater things than these, because I am going to my Father.
16:20	You will weep and mourn while the world rejoices. You will grieve, but your grief will turn to joy.
16:23	My Father will give you whatever you ask in my name.

21:18   When you were younger you dressed yourself and went where you wanted, but when you are old you will stretch out your hands, and someone else will dress you and lead you where you do not want to go.

7. What Else?

Perhaps the reader wants to study the other Gospels, the Acts, or the Epistles. If this is the case we are most pleased, but we do ask all to continue to read the Scriptures and not, now having come to the end of this book, to put their Bible back on the shelf to gather dust. Please remember the Christian life is from faith to faith i.e. to a deeper personal knowledge of the Lord Jesus Christ. Failure to grow physically in natural life is sad and so is failure to grow in Spiritual life.

Please continue to read books but remember the Berean attitude and check to see if what people say is true. We all make mistakes and none of us is infallible. Please continue to read Scripture and remember:

> "Do your best to present yourself to God as one approved,
> a workman who does not need to be ashamed
> who correctly handles the word of truth"
> (2 Timothy 2:15).

More on John's Gospel

 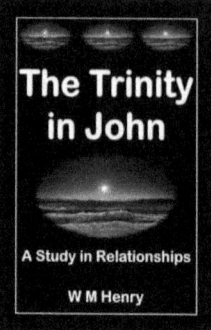 

That you may believe: The Eight Signs in John's Gospel
By Charles Ozanne

The Trinity in John: A Study in Relationships
By W M Henry

The Upper Room Discourse: John13-17
By W M Henry

John: His life and writings
By Michael Penny

Further details of the above books can be seen on **www.obt.org.uk**

They can be ordered from that website and also from:

The Open Bible Trust,
Fordland Mount, Upper Basildon,
Reading, RG8 8LU, UK.

They are also available as eBooks from Amazon and Apple and as KDP paperbacks from Amazon.

About the Author

Michael Penny was born in Ebbw Vale, Gwent, Wales in 1943. He read Mathematics at the University of Reading, before teaching for twelve years and becoming the Director of Mathematics and Business Studies at Queen Mary's College Basingstoke in Hampshire, England. In 1978 he entered Christian publishing, and in 1984 became the administrator of the Open Bible Trust.

He held this position for seven years, before moving to the USA and becoming pastor of Grace Church in New Berlin, Wisconsin. He returned to Britain in 1999, and is at present the Administrator and Editor of The Open Bible Trust. In 2010 he was elected Chairman of Churches Together in Reading, where he speaks in a number of churches. He is a member of the Advisory Committee to Reading University Christian Union and is a chaplain at Reading College, and has helped set up chaplaincy teams in a number of other colleges.

He lives between Reading and Oxford, in West Berkshire, with his wife and has appeared on BBC Radio Berkshire and Premier Radio a number of times. He has made several speaking tours of America, Canada, Australia, New Zealand and the Netherlands, as well as ones to South Africa and the Philippines. Some of his writings have been translated into German and Russian.

As well as editing and writing articles for *Search* magazine and many Bible study booklets, he has also written several major books including *40 Problem Passages; Approaching the Bible; The Bible! Myth or Message?; Galatians - Interpretation and Application; Joel's Prophecy; Past and Future; The Miracles of the Apostles; Questions and Queries about Christianity; Questions and Queries about the New Testament; Introducing God's Word* (with Carol Brown and Lynn Mrotek); *Introducing God's Plan* (with Sylvia Penny).

He has written two books with W M Henry

- *Following Philippians*, which is ideal for Post-Alpha groups
- *The Will of God: Past and Present.*

His latest books are:

- *James; His Life and Letter*
- *Paul: A Missionary of Genius*
- *Peter: His life and letters*
- *John: His life and writings*

Details of these books, and other writings, can be seen at

www.obt.org.uk

* * * * * * * * * * * * * * * * * * *

Michael Penny is editor of *Search* magazine

For a free sample of
The Open Bible Trust's magazine *Search*,
please email

admin@obt.org.uk

or visit

www.obt.org.uk/search

www.ingramcontent.com/pod-product-compliance
Lightning Source LLC
Chambersburg PA
CBHW071516040426
42444CB00008B/1672